Our Amazing Bodies

Our Amazing Bodies

A Supplement to Childcraft—
The How and Why Library

World Book, Inc.
a Scott Fetzer company
Chicago London Sydney Toronto

World Book, Inc.
525 W. Monroe
Chicago, IL 60661

ISBN 0-7166-0695-X
Library of Congress Catalog Card No. 65-25105
Printed in the United States of America

1 2 3 4 5 6 7 8 9 10 99 98 97 96 95

Contents

Touring Your Lungs and Heart 82

Your Breathing Machine ◆ Body basics: What Caused That Bloody Nose? ◆ Air Alert! ◆ Body basics: How Do You Speak Up? ◆ The Heart of the Matter ◆ Body science: Putting Your Pulse on Paper ◆ A Closer Look at Blood ◆ SomeBody you should know: Charles Drew ◆ Exploring Your Circulatory System ◆ Body basics: How Do Cuts Stop Bleeding? ◆ Fighters for Your Life

The Great Digestion Works 110

Gateway to Digestion ◆ Body basics: Why Do Teeth Get Cavities? ◆ Down the Hatch ◆ SomeBody you should know: William Beaumont ◆ The Great Food Breakdown ◆ Body science: Soaking It Up ◆ Your Body's Waterworks

Calling Brain Central 134

Being Brainy ◆ Your Nerve Networks ◆ Body basics: Are You a Lefty or a Righty? ◆ Your Brain Works the Night Shift ◆ The Night Chant ◆ SomeBody you should know: Sigmund Freud ◆ Sense Alert ◆ Body science: Catch the Tiger and All Ears

Staff

Preface

What are you made of? Sugar and spice? All that's nice? Frogs and snails and puppy-dogs' tails? Guess again!

You're made of incredible wonders from the top of your head—which is probably covered by about 100,000 hairs—to the tips of your toes—which have nails that completely grow out about every eight months!

Our bodies are indeed amazing, often raising many thoughtful questions.

Why do you have blood?

Why is it not just rude, but potentially dangerous, to talk with your mouth full?

How many bones make up your skeleton?

Why does your nose grow in the middle of your face instead of under your left arm?

What do your voice and fingerprints have in common!

How does your brain signal your body to start and stop growing?

How big an area would your skin cover if you could peel it all off and roll it out FLAT?

You don't have to ask a grown-up for the answers to these questions—just look inside these pages. You'll get the facts, play some games, and meet some lively characters as you discover just how amazing your one and only body truly is!

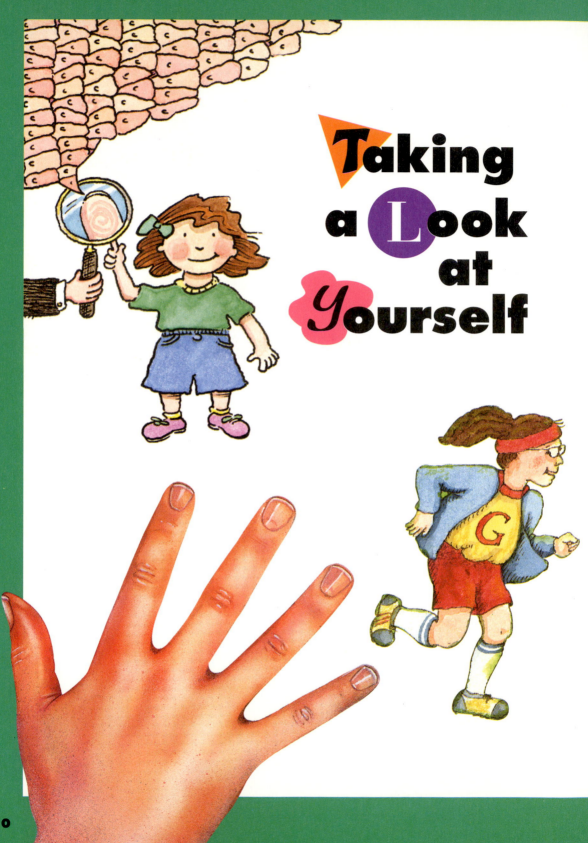

Taking a Look at Yourself

Do you jump like a frog, sing like a bird, swim like a fish, climb like a monkey, or calculate like a computer? Or is it the other way around—do they jump, sing, swim, climb, and compute like you? No matter, nothing else is exactly like the human body. Just take a look at yourself and all your wonderful features.

What Is Your Body?

Your body . . .

. . . is made up of tiny parts called cells, most of which can be seen only under a microscope. A human body has about 500 times more cells than the Milky Way has known stars.

. . . is mostly water—between 55 and 75 percent. The water in a grown-up's body could almost fill eleven 1-gallon (3.8-liter) jugs.

. . . is full of metals and minerals. For example, a healthy human body contains enough iron to make a 1-inch (2.5-centimeter) nail and more calcium than 2 pounds (.9 kilogram) of chalk.

. . . runs on fuel. Its fuel is food instead of gasoline. If you eat three meals a day and live seventy-five years, you will have eaten more than 82,000 meals.

. . . works on a schedule. A built-in clock wakes you at the same time almost every morning. Another built-in clock releases a chemical that makes your body grow. It shuts off the chemical when you reach your full height.

. . . has more than a dozen systems working together. When you scratch, for example, you use at least four body systems. Your nervous system tells you where you itch, your muscle and skeletal systems move your hand, and your fingernails—part of your skin—do the scratching.

. . . is built to last a long time. One of the oldest people on record lived almost 121 years.

BODYscience

Learn About Your Body

Ready to investigate your body? Play this game by yourself or with a friend. Begin by placing your button on START. Then flip the coin. If it comes up heads, advance one space. If it turns up tails, advance two spaces. If you land on a space with instructions, follow the directions. Then it's your friend's turn.

Count how many places your thumb can bend.

Describe a dream you had recently. Then move ahead one space.

START

Put your hand on your bellybutton, then move your hand up and to the side. Can you feel your ribcage?

Pat your head with one hand while you rub circles on your stomach with the other.

If you can't kiss your elbow, go back three spaces.

Watch a clock with a second hand and count the number of breaths you take in one minute.

Look at something far away. Then hold a finger in front of one eye. If you can't clearly focus on both the faraway object and your finger at the same time, move back one space.

14

Describe the surface of your tongue in one word.

Name your two favorite smells.

Press your palms against your ears. Can you hear your blood rushing?

Touch the tips of your ring fingers and fold down your other fingers. Now put your knuckles and palms together and try to move your ring fingers apart.

FINISH

Keep reading to find out more about *How Your Body Works!*

Try out the muscles that wiggle your ears. Can you make them move your ears? Not everyone can.

Look at your palm while it's flat. Then cup your hand. Explain what you see.

Touch your toes. Then jump ahead one space.

Feel the bone that runs from your little-finger side of your wrist to your elbow—that's your ulna. Then move ahead to the skeleton.

Body Teamwork

Organ, muscle, nerve, and bone—
body parts seldom act alone.
They pull together as a team—
to help you work and play and dream.

Gretchen's leg muscles
lift, and her heart
muscles pump;
they help her to skip,
and they help her
to jump.

Ollie's arm muscles pull as
he flips upside down;
his inner ears help him land
straight on the ground.

Yuri's body heats up as
he jogs across town,
but his skin glands are
sweating to keep him
cooled down.

Dawn's muscles lift, and
her joints turn about,
to help her throw the
soccer ball out.

Otto's spine stretches—
his back muscles, too—
as he does bends and twists
that some people can't do.

Bella's broken leg itches and
aches while it heals—
her bone cells are
growing; her nerve
cells can feel.

Paul's jaw opens and closes—
 his tongue wiggles, too—
when he tells all his friends
 what he's planning to do.

Andy's nerves go to work—
 his nose sniffs as well—
so the cells in his brain
 can make out that odd smell.

Rosa's stomach keeps mixing
 whatever she munches;
it's pouring out juice to digest
 her school lunches.

Visitors
O
Home
O

Theo's eardrums hear rhythms,
and nerves tell his feet,
how to keep time
to a fast Latin beat.

Sara's brain sends
signals as she thinks,
and her hand writes her
thoughts in pencil or
ink.

Gina's skull keeps her brain
safe at work and at play;
she can dream, she can think,
every night, every day.

GO BODY

Oscar's muscles focus
the lens in each eye,
as he watches geese
flying in the sky.

And everything these body parts do,
your body part team can do for you.

GO, BODY PARTS, GO!

O PARTS GO!

What Makes Human Bodies Special?

Hi! I'm Zack, a zoologist. Welcome to the Animal Cracker Zoo. Let's start our tour with the apes. You'll have to excuse them if they sit while we stand. Apes can't stay standing upright. Most of the time they swing by their arms or walk on their hands and feet. We humans have unique spine, buttocks, and leg structures that allow us to stand upright all day. An ape's spine curves like an archer's bow, so apes stand and walk hunched over. A human spine curves like an *S*. The curve of the lower back holds the rest of the spine upright. Also, apes

Ape skeleton

Human skeleton

have longer arms than legs and can use their feet for grasping. We humans have longer legs than arms and use our feet mainly for support.

The researcher over there is trying to communicate with a dolphin. The dolphin, like many other animals, uses various sounds to express emotion or simple messages. But humans use language. We can talk about the lunch we had today or about something that happened hundreds of years ago.

Do you like bugs? The Arthropod House has lots of them. Many bugs have only a small group of nerve cells for a brain. Some other animals have large, complex brains. But humans have the most highly developed brain of all. This makes us able to solve more difficult problems than other animals can. Human bodies can dance and swim, but it was human brains that figured out how to build airplanes so that humans could fly.

23

How do opposable thumbs make humans special? Get some tape and find out. Tape your thumbs to the palms of your hands. Then try daily tasks such as buttoning a shirt or tying a shoe. Not easy, is it? Without these thumbs, some tasks are just about impossible.

See the squirrels holding their food? That reminds me of another unusual feature of humans. Humans, as well as many other primates, have hands with *opposable thumbs* for grasping; squirrels don't. Opposable thumbs come in handy for making and using tools.

Oh look, here comes Sara with food for the animals. It's time for your dinner too. Please come back soon for another tour of the Animal Cracker Zoo.

Some**B**O**d**Y you should know

A NDREAS V ESALIUS

Have you sometimes wondered if doctors ever mistake a liver for an appendix? The answer is "not likely," because medical students *dissect* (cut up) dead bodies and study their parts. The person who made dissection common in medical schools was Andreas Vesalius (ahn DRAY uhs vih SAY lee uhs).

Born in 1514 into a family of physicians, Andreas also studied medicine. In 1537 he became a professor at the University of Padua in Italy. It was the best medical school in Europe. At that time, a human *cadaver* (dead body) was dissected only once in a while. The best information about the human body was from Galen, who had written about it hundreds of years earlier. This physician had described the insides of monkeys, pigs, and other animals to show what the inside of a human body was probably like.

However, Andreas believed that doing careful, thorough dissections of human cadavers was the only way to properly teach human anatomy. He used cadavers often and dissected them as he taught his students. From these dissections, he soon realized that Galen was wrong about many things— for instance, the shape of the human skeleton and the positions and functions of some human organs.

Andreas used his knowledge to write *On the Structure of the Human Body,* the first book on human anatomy with clear and detailed pictures. Published in 1543, the book was illustrated with beautiful drawings of the muscles, bones, and internal organs. This work made Andreas famous, but more important, it helped make the study of human anatomy accurate.

Andreas Vesalius made the dissection of cadavers common in medical schools.

Old-fashioned Body Care

Dear Customer:

With this issue of our Body Care Catalog, we bring you the results of centuries of research and invention—the best body care products of earlier times. We're sure you'll enjoy and appreciate these helpful items, from Phoenician soap to ancient Egyptian toothbrushes. Place your order today!

Yours truly,
The Body Care Staff

20% OFF
METAL MIRRORS
∞

Get in on the most popular grooming fad ever! For centuries, metal was the last word in mirrors. Now you can own an exact replica of the mirrors used by Sumerians 5,500 years ago. Made of highly polished bronze, the mirror is set in your choice of a wood, ivory, or gold handle.

EGYPTIAN "CHEW STICK" THE ORIGINAL TOOTHBRUSH

~

Produced as early as 3000 B.C., the chew stick is a pencil-slim twig with a frayed end much like a paintbrush. Buy yours while the supply lasts and brush like an ancient Egyptian.

THE FIRST WORD IN TOOTHPASTE ~

Wake up with a pucker when you use the toothpaste of the pharaohs. Early Egyptians dissolved the mineral natron (NAY tron) in water and applied it to their teeth with their chew sticks. They even used natron to mummify (preserve) the bodies of their dead. Early Romans also used natron. They burned it and rubbed it on their teeth to whiten them. Please specify Egyptian or Roman when ordering toothpaste.

LATHER UP WITH GOAT FAT

Known chiefly as sailors, Phoenicians from the eastern Mediterranean brought the first soap to Europe. Our own Phoenician soap is made from their 2,600-year-old recipe. We boil the purest water, the finest ashes, and the richest goat fat until they form a waxy solid just like the kind the people in the ancient kingdom of Phoenicia used for washing.

Each box contains three ship-shaped bars.

KEEP YOUR HAIR SCUM-FREE

Shampoo was born in the early 1900's after German chemists discovered these detergents. Detergents remove oil from hair without depositing soap scum. Now you can wash your hair with the same detergent-based shampoo formula that may have cleaned great-great-grandmother's hair.

Buy two and get one free.

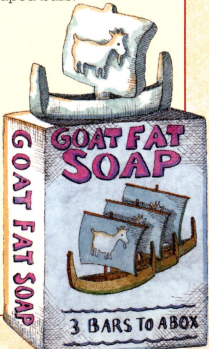

𝕽edecorating?

In 1775, Alexander Cummings patented the modern flush toilet, and beginning in the 1880's, architects included bathrooms in the new houses they designed. Let us redo your bathroom with fixtures like this British original.

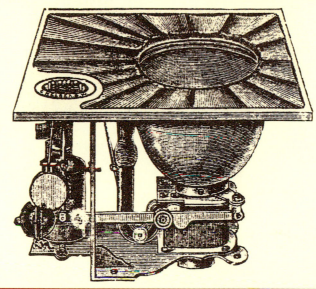

HAIR TO DYE FOR

Early Romans favored black hair. So they boiled walnut shells and onionlike plants called leeks to make dark hair dye. Now, you too can make your hair black with the dye Romans used long ago.

Caution: This strong dye may make your hair fall out.

All our body care products are guaranteed. If you are not pleased for any reason, return your order for a full refund. No questions asked.

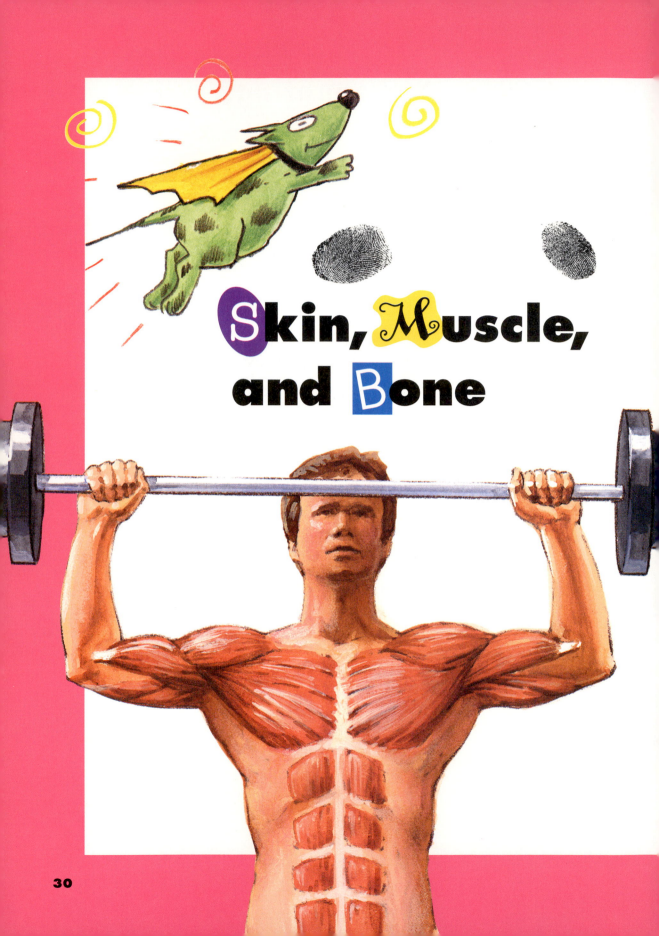

Skin, Muscle, and Bone

They support. They protect you. Without them, you'd be no more than a glob of goo on the ground. We're not talking about your parents. We're talking about your skin, muscles, and bones. Muscles move you and move things through you. Bones are the frame your muscles hang on and the protective armor for your important organs. Skin wraps your body in a neat package, helping protect what's inside.

Captain Dermis

Not long ago, Jo Jo Johnson was a makeup mixer in a cosmetics factory—that is, until he learned of a plot to ruin the world's lotion supply. Thrown into a bubbling vat of sunscreen by the factory boss's dreaded henchmen, the Pimple Boys, Jo Jo was left for dead. Days later and far from dead, Jo Jo emerged, transformed into a being with superhuman strength and a glowing complexion. He became . . .

CAPTAIN DERMIS

AND HIS DOG Flex

Hello, readers. Many people doubt the powers of a superhero named Captain Dermis and the importance of skin. I'm here to put those doubts to rest once and for all.

Skin may look simple, but it's more complex than you'd think. It's made up of three layers. The outer layer, called the *epidermis* (EHP uh DUHR mihs), is generally about as thin as a piece of paper. Most of your skin's growth occurs in this layer. Tiny living elements called *cells* form in the lower part of the epidermis and then gradually get pushed upward. As they move

33

toward the surface, they begin to die off and become tough, flat, dry, and nearly waterproof.

Right under the epidermis is the layer called the *dermis.* Your dermis is much thicker than your epidermis—up to 40 times as thick. It's main parts include blood vessels and nerve endings. Your dermis also contains the skin's important structures—the sweat glands, oil glands, and small pits or sacs called *follicles* (FAH luh kulz), where hair grows. These structures are actually formed from parts of epidermis cells that reach down into the dermis.

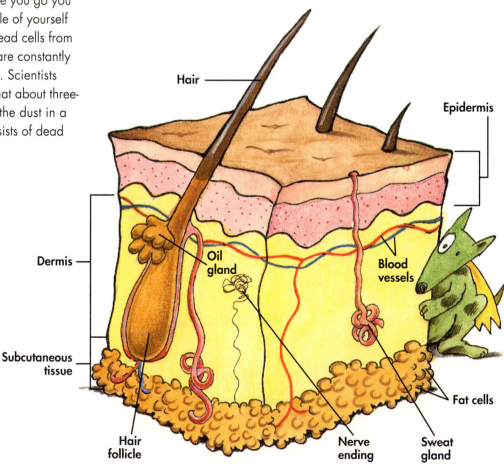

Hair

Epidermis

Dermis

Subcutaneous tissue

Oil gland

Blood vessels

Hair follicle

Nerve ending

Sweat gland

Fat cells

34

Under your dermis is the *subcutaneous tissue* (SUHB kyoo TAYN ee uhs TIHSH yoo). This layer contains fat cells, other connecting and supporting tissue, and blood vessels.

Skin has many qualities important to a superhero. First of all, skin is strong and flexible. It is also very nearly waterproof. If you had no skin, the vital fluids in your body would evaporate. In no time at all, you would look like a dried-up piece of shoe leather. And imagine what would happen if your skin couldn't keep water out. Every time you took a bath or went swimming, your cells would absorb water. You would swell up like a sponge.

Skin keeps other unwanted things out, such as harmful bacteria and viruses that can make you sick. It's an important part of your body's *immune system,* which fights all kinds of harmful invaders.

Your skin also helps protect your body temperature. When you're in danger of overheating, blood vessels in your skin *dilate* (expand) to throw off excess heat. Your skin allows the heat to be released as sweat, cooling your body down. On the other hand, the fat in your subcutaneous tissue helps keep you warm. And it acts like a cushion too, protecting your body against bumps.

Skin absorbs the sun's ultraviolet light. Your body can use these light rays to make vitamin D.

So you see, I have many reasons to be proud to wear the symbol of the skin. But now, I must excuse myself. My nose itches—that's my special signal. It tells me that someone somewhere needs help.

People may not come in as many colors as jellybeans or flowers or crayons. But human beings have a wide variety of skin shades.

Whatever shade your skin is, it comes from a substance called *melanin* (MEHL uh nihn). Melanin is a brown *pigment* (coloring). It is produced inside cells called *melanocytes* (MEHL uh nuh syts), which are in skin, hair, and eyes.

All people, no matter how light or dark their skin is, have about the same number of melanocytes. But different people's cells produce different amounts of melanin.

Basically, the less melanin produced, the lighter the skin. The melanocytes of light-skinned people produce less melanin than those of dark-skinned people. Darker shades of skin also have more melanin closer to the surface of the skin. People with yellowish skin have a pigment called *carotene* (KAIR uh teen) in addition to melanin.

Sometimes people have darker areas of skin, or spots, called freckles. These spots are caused by increased amounts, or clumps, of melanin.

The amount of melanin produced in each person is mainly determined by *heredity*—traits you inherit from your parents. However, melanocytes also produce more melanin when exposed to the sun, causing the skin to tan. The body produces more melanin to help protect the skin from sunburn and skin cancer caused by ultraviolet light. But any skin that is exposed to too much ultraviolet light eventually burns.

Each person's skin has a coloring called melanin.

BO**d**y**science**

Study Your Own Fingerprints

THINGS YOU NEED:

- 2 sheets of paper
- a piece of soft charcoal, a charcoal pencil, or a soft (#1) pencil
- wide, transparent tape
- a magnifying glass

This activity is easiest to do with a partner.

1. Rub the charcoal or pencil lead on several places on one sheet of paper to make dark patches.

2. If your hands are messy after doing *step 1,* wash and dry them.

3. Rub one finger on one of the charcoal or pencil patches.

4. Have your partner stick a piece of tape on the end of your charcoal- or lead-covered finger. Then have your partner peel the tape off carefully and stick it on the other sheet of paper.

5. Repeat *steps 3* and *4* with your other fingers.

Examine your fingerprints with the magnifying glass. Look at the diagrams on this page. Which patterns do you have? Make prints of your partner's fingers. Compare them with yours.

From Your Hair to Your Toenails

Are you looking at my hair? Good! I want it to attract attention. I'm the lead singer in the group The Weeds. You probably know hair doesn't grow out of a person's head in this shade of green. And it doesn't stick up like this all by itself. It takes work, but it's worth it. People notice. When I think of all the fuss people make about my hairdo, I laugh. I mean, hairs are only strands of hardened, dead skin cells. Nails also are made of layers of hardened, dead skin cells.

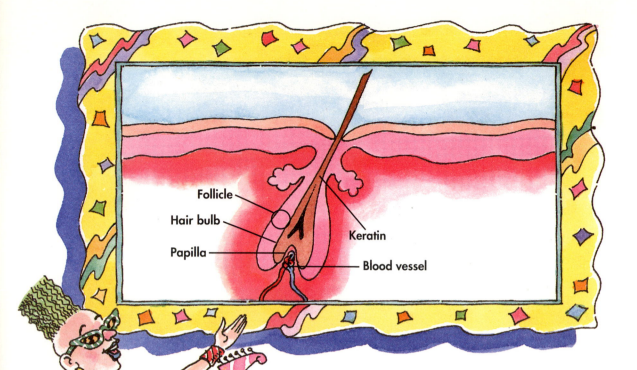

Follicle

Hair bulb

Papilla

Keratin

Blood vessel

BODY LANGUAGE

Keratin is hard protein that forms when certain kinds of cells die. It is a main part of hair, nails, and animals' claws, hoofs, horns, scales, and feathers.

Hairs grow in the dermis in little pits or sacs called *follicles*. Each hair begins as a group of living, dividing cells. These cells grow from a soft, rounded *hair bulb*. The hair bulb surrounds a tiny knob called a *papilla* (puh PIHL luh), which has blood vessels that nourish the new cells. As the new cells grow, they push up the older cells, which form hard layers of a substance called *keratin* (KEHR uh tuhn), and the hair grows longer. See my nails? They form the same way my hair does. New cells form under the skin in the *matrix*. They push older cells forward to make the *plate,* or nail. The part of the hair and nail that we see and admire is deader than a doornail!

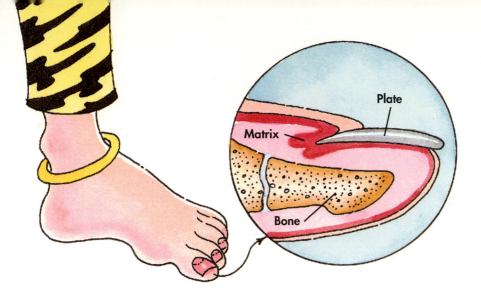

Hair color comes from melanin—that's the same pigment that makes skin brown. Blondes have very little melanin in their hair, and red-haired people have a pigment called *phaeomelanin* (FEE oh MEHL uh nihn). Curls? That's another story. They depend on the shape of your hair—the flatter the strands of hair, the curlier they are. Straight hairs are round.

Hairs on your body grow for a certain length of time. Then they fall out, and the follicles go into a resting phase. After the resting phase, the follicles start to grow new hairs. The hair on a person's head has the longest growing phase. That's why some people can grow their hair really long. Other hairs—eyelashes for example—have a short growing phase, so on most people they never get longer than about 1/4 inch (.6 centimeter). The hair on your head can grow approximately 1/2 inch (1.25 centimeters) every month.

I'll let you in on a secret: My hair is really straight, and it's just plain old brown. So I see my hairdresser, Jacob, often. He explained to me that hair is made up of three layers: the *medulla*—that's the soft inner part; the *cuticle,* which is the tough, scaly outside; and the *cortex,* the layer between them. The cuticle on healthy, shiny hair has flat, overlapping cells.

mih DOOL uh
KOHR tehks
KYOO tuh kuhl

Medulla

Cortex

Cuticle

Even if it looks like green hay, my hair does what it's supposed to do. Hair doesn't just make someone look good. It also protects the body's precious brain from cold air and too much of the sun's heat, and even from being bumped. Hairs on other parts of your body are important, too. For example, the hairs inside your nose trap dust and other tiny materials that could

hurt your lungs. Eyelashes and eyebrows help protect your eyes from sunlight and from dust and other particles. Many of the hairs on other parts of your body can actually help you sense the world around you. These hairs are connected to nerve endings. When something brushes against them, they let your brain know—fast!

I see you are admiring my hair. I can get you an appointment with Jacob if you like—but promise not to get the same hairdo.

Muscle Talk

It's not often we muscles get a chance to take a break. But the human we belong to is asleep, so a few of us decided to get together for a little rest and relaxation.

Actually, most of the muscles resting now are *skeletal* (SKEHL uh tuhl) muscles. We're the muscles that you can feel—and sometimes see—right under the skin, the ones that give you much of your shape. Our main job is helping you move your body, but you use us even when you're standing still. The reason we're called *skeletal* muscles is because we hold the bones of your skeleton together. We're also called *voluntary* muscles because you can control our movements.

You might not know about the other muscles—the *involuntary* muscles—because they are deep inside you. They get their name because you don't consciously control them. They work all day and night to keep your organ systems operating.

Some of your major voluntary muscles are shown at the right. But you have many more—including some on your backside and small ones in your face, hands, and feet that move your eyelids, jaw, fingers, and toes.

Brachioradialis
(BRAY kee aw
RAY dee AL ihs)

Biceps (BY sehps)

Triceps (TRY sehps)

Deltoid (DEHL toyd)

Vastus lateralis
(VAS tuhs LAT uhr AH lihs)

Adductor longus
(ad DUHK tuhr
LONG uhs)

Vastus medialis
(VAS tuhs
MEE dee AH lihs)

Gracilis
(GRAS uh lihs)

Tibialis anterior
(TIHB ee AH lihs
an TEER ee uhr)

Flexor carpi radialis
(FLEHK suhr KAHR py
RAY dee AH lihs)

Pectoralis major
(PEHK tuh RAHL ihs MAY juhr)

Serratus anterior
(suhr RA tuhs an TEER ee uhr)

Rectus abdominis
(REHK tuhs ab DAHM uh nihs)

External oblique
(ehk STUHR nuhl o BLEEK)

Rectus femorus
(REHK tuhs FEHM uhr uhs)

Sartorius
(sahr TOHR ee uhs)

**Extensor digitorum
longus**
(ehk STEHN suhr
DIHJ ih TOHR uhm
LONG us)

Soleus
(SOH lee uhs)

What's the difference between voluntary and involuntary muscles? Mainly, it's how we look and the way we move. All muscles are made of long, thin cells called *fibers*. Skeletal muscles like me are made up of fibers that have light and dark bands called *striations* (stry AY shuhnz). When you want to move, our fibers *contract* (kuhn TRAKT), or get shorter and thicker, very quickly.

BODY LANGUAGE

Some muscles' names may seem complicated. But with these translations, you'll see just what they mean.

external: on or to the side
lateralis: to the side
longus: long
medialis: near the middle
oblique: slanting
radialis: relates to the radius bone in the forearm
rectus: straight
vastus: big or vast

45

Skeletal muscles may work involuntarily in what are called *reflex actions*. For example, when something gets near your eye, you automatically blink. Other reflexes cause you to jerk your hand away from something hot or sharp.

Skeletal muscles, such as biceps, have bands called striations.

We skeletal muscles have different kinds of fibers for the different ways you use us. If you jog long distances, we mainly use our *slow twitch* fibers. Slow twitch fibers use oxygen efficiently, so we can keep you on the move for long periods of time. *Fast twitch* fibers are for jumping or doing pushups or other activities that require short bursts of energy.

Most involuntary muscles don't have striations. We call these involuntary muscles *smooth* muscles. Smooth muscles work in the lining of your blood vessels, intestines, bladder, and other hollow organs. I don't want to call

Smooth muscles are mostly found deep inside your body, as in the stomach.

Cardiac muscle, found only in the heart, has striations but is involuntary muscle.

them lazy—after all, they work long hours—but they contract slowly compared to us skeletal muscles. For example, smooth muscles in your stomach contract in wavelike motions. They churn up the food you eat and push it into the small intestine.

But it's the heart, or cardiac (KAHR dee ak), muscle that you really have to admire. *Cardiac muscle* has an important job—it's responsible for keeping your heart beating. Cardiac muscle tissue is strong. It has striations that are a lot like skeletal muscle, but it's also involuntary muscle that contracts automatically, like smooth muscle tissue.

Whoa! We're getting the signal to roll over. I guess we can do that. See, even we skeletal muscles put in a little overtime.

BODY BULLETIN

Your body's longest muscle is the *sartorius*, which runs from the outside of your hip to the inside of your knee. Your smallest muscle is the tiny *stapedius* (stuh PEE dee uhs) in each ear.

47

Movin' Around

BODY BULLETIN

Are you one of the few people who can wiggle their ears? If so, you do it by contracting the *auricular* (aw RIHK yuh luhr) muscles. These muscles connect certain bones and tissues of the skull to the outside of the ear.

In Studio A, the Kidaerobics class is in full swing. Imagine that you can peer under their skin to see how their muscles work.

Most skeletal muscles work in pairs. One muscle can pull a bone one way, and its partner can pull it another way. For example, when the kids bend and straighten one arm in time to the music, they are using mainly the two upper-arm muscles: the *biceps* on one side of the arm and the *triceps* on the other. When the arm bends, the biceps contracts, and the triceps relaxes. The contraction pulls up on one of the lower-arm bones, and the elbow bends. When the arm straightens, the biceps relaxes, and the triceps muscle contracts.

Can you see that the skeletal muscles all have similar parts? Most are joined to bones by strong cords called *tendons*. In most skeletal muscles, one end is attached to a bone that doesn't move when the muscle contracts. This end is called the *head,* and the place it is attached to is called the *origin* of the muscle. The middle part of the muscle is the *belly*. The other end of the muscle is attached to the bone that the muscle moves. That place of attachment is called the *insertion* (ihn SUHR shuhn).

Whew! Those kids are working up a sweat. Such vigorous, heart-pumping exercise improves the muscles' ability to produce energy. As a result, the muscles can work for longer periods of time.

Biceps relaxed

Trapezius (truh PEE zee uhs)

Origin of biceps

Head of biceps

Belly of biceps

Biceps contracted

Triceps contracted

Insertion of biceps

Skeletal muscles work in pairs. For example, the biceps and triceps work to bend and straighten your arm.

Triceps relaxed

Latissimus dorsi (luh TIHS ih muhs DOHR sy)

Adults sometimes use exercise equipment to help keep their muscles strong or to make their muscles grow bigger.

To keep muscles strong and to make them grow bigger, people need to specifically work their different muscle groups. People need to work each group by pushing or pulling against something. Let's visit Studio B, where you can see men and women using weights and special machines. This isn't a room for kids to use, though. Weightlifting can cause serious injury to muscles that aren't fully grown.

When you look at a person who lifts weights regularly—especially a bodybuilder—you can really see the shape of the muscles. The big shoulder muscles of a bodybuilder are the *deltoids*. They attach the upper-arm bone to the collarbone. The bulging chest is courtesy of the *pectorals*. But you don't have to be a weightlifter to know how it feels to build muscles. If you have ever moved a toy chest or tried to pick up your bicycle, then you know how it feels to make your muscles work hard.

Now, let's have our muscles move us to Studio C. A gymnast there is holding a handstand. As he pauses, motionless, you may not realize he's

BODY LANGUAGE

Ligaments (LIHG uh muhnts) are strong, fiberlike tissues that bind bones together at the joints. People who are unusually limber have very flexible ligaments.

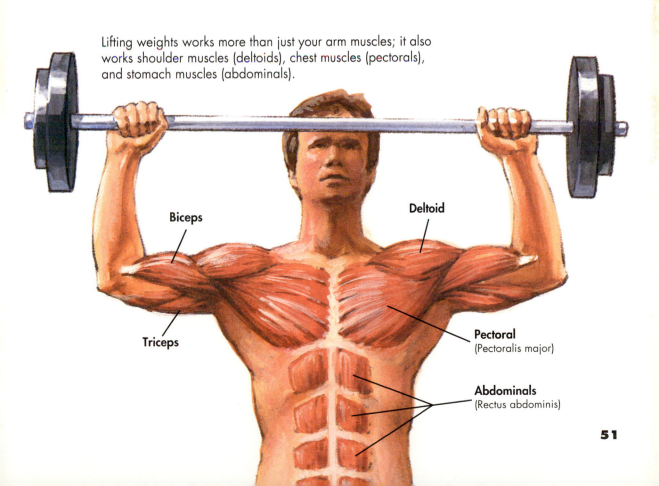

Lifting weights works more than just your arm muscles; it also works shoulder muscles (deltoids), chest muscles (pectorals), and stomach muscles (abdominals).

Biceps

Triceps

Deltoid

Pectoral
(Pectoralis major)

Abdominals
(Rectus abdominis)

using his muscles, but he is. His arms are strongly contracted to support the weight of his body. And the muscles of his shoulders, legs, back, and stomach are constantly making tiny adjustments that keep his body balanced.

Groups of large muscles in your legs and buttocks help you kick. Your gastrocnemius makes up most of your calf.

Quadriceps
(KWAHD ruh sehps)

Gluteus maximus
(GLOO tee uhs MAKS uh muhs)

Hamstring group

Gastrocnemius
(GAS trohk NEE mee uhs)

BODY BULLETIN

The gluteus maximus muscles in the buttocks are among your strongest and heaviest muscles.

The girl across the studio is practicing martial arts. When she kicks, she is using two groups of thigh muscles—the *quadriceps* group on the front and the *hamstring* group on the back. She can kick high because she has properly stretched her muscles, tendons, and ligaments every day. When you're *flexible*, your muscles can more easily move through their full range of motion.

Well, I hope you have clearly seen how muscles can help you move in many different ways. Next time, bring your gym bag so you can give *your* muscles a workout.

J ACKIE J OYNER - K ERSEE

Running, jumping, and throwing—that's how Jackie Joyner-Kersee became one of the world's greatest athletes. Jackie's sport, the *heptathlon* (hehp TATH lon), is a series of seven events—the 100-meter hurdles, the high jump, the shot-put, the 200-meter dash, the long jump, the javelin throw, and the 800-meter run. Athletes compete in the events over the course of two days.

As a schoolgirl in East St. Louis, Illinois, Jackie fell in love with the long jump. She competed in her first track meet at the age of nine and finished last. But before long, she was bringing home "firsts."

Jackie brought home her passion for jumping, too. She liked to practice by leaping off the front porch. Soon, other kids were helping her carry sand home from the nearby youth center in potato-chip bags to make a landing pit. In high school, she became a basketball and volleyball star and set a state long-jump record.

But in college at the University of California at Los Angeles, Jackie discovered the sport that would make her famous. A coach at the university, Bob Kersee, recognized that Jackie's athletic talent was broad enough for her to take on the demanding heptathlon. Jackie married Bob in 1986 and went on to become a star athlete in the heptathlon.

As a competitor in the heptathlon, Jackie had to excel in many areas of athletic performance. She trained for competition six days a week, combining strength-building workouts with speed training and heart-pumping aerobic exercises. She also practiced the complicated motions involved in her throwing and jumping events.

Jackie became the first woman to win the Olympic heptathlon championship twice in a row. She won gold medals in the 1988 and 1992 Olympics and set the world record for total points in the event at the 1988 games. She is a heroine of the heptathlon.

Jackie Joyner-Kersee

How 'Bout Them Bones?

Boo! Did I scare you? No? How about if I shake my hands at you—clackety-clack? No? Oh well! I guess even though I'm a skeleton, you can tell I'm a nice guy.

My name is Thurston Funnybones, and I live in this dusty old closet. I understand you want to learn about bones, and I can tell you! Scientists divide bones into four groups, depending on their shape. *Long bones* are the bones of your arms, legs, fingers, and toes. The rest of the bones in your body are *short bones,* such as those in your wrists and ankles; *flat bones,* like your skull, kneecaps, shoulder blades, and ribs; or *irregular bones,* which include those in your spine and your face.

Surrounding your bones is a thin covering called the *periosteum* (PEHR ee AHS tee uhm). The periosteum has blood vessels and nerve endings. The blood vessels carry food to bone cells. The nerve endings let you know if a bone is injured by sending pain signals to your brain.

BODY LANGUAGE

Funny bone isn't really the name of a bone. It's a place in the elbow where a nerve that runs from the spine into the hand is unprotected. When you bump it, you get a strange, funny feeling. It's probably named after one of the bones the nerve passes over–the humerus.

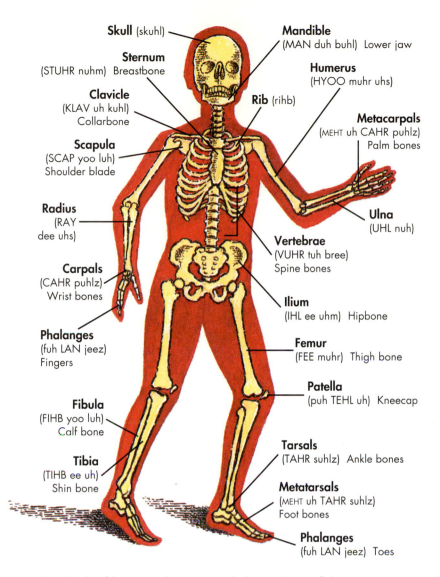

Skull (skuhl)

Sternum
(STUHR nuhm) Breastbone

Clavicle
(KLAV uh kuhl)
Collarbone

Scapula
(SCAP yoo luh)
Shoulder blade

Radius
(RAY
dee uhs)

Carpals
(CAHR puhlz)
Wrist bones

Phalanges
(fuh LAN jeez)
Fingers

Fibula
(FIHB yoo luh)
Calf bone

Tibia
(TIHB ee uh)
Shin bone

Mandible
(MAN duh buhl) Lower jaw

Humerus
(HYOO muhr uhs)

Rib (rihb)

Metacarpals
(MEHT uh CAHR puhlz)
Palm bones

Ulna
(UHL nuh)

Vertebrae
(VUHR tuh bree)
Spine bones

Ilium
(IHL ee uhm) Hipbone

Femur
(FEE muhr) Thigh bone

Patella
(puh TEHL uh) Kneecap

Tarsals
(TAHR suhlz) Ankle bones

Metatarsals
(MEHT uh TAHR suhlz)
Foot bones

Phalanges
(fuh LAN jeez) Toes

Hundreds of bones make up your skeleton. Some of the major ones are shown here with their common names.

Compact bone magnified
hundreds of times its size

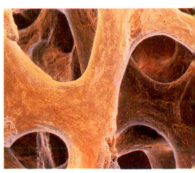

Cancellous bone magnified
about thirty times its size

Bones themselves can be of two kinds of tissue. *Compact bone* is the hard, solid outer bone. It is as strong as iron but much lighter in weight. *Cancellous* (CAN suh luhs) bone is found inside the compact tissue of most long bones. Cancellous bone has lots of tiny empty pockets, somewhat like a hardened sponge.

BODY BULLETIN

The smallest bone in your body is the stirrup bone inside each ear. The bone is about 1/10 inch (.25 cm) long.

55

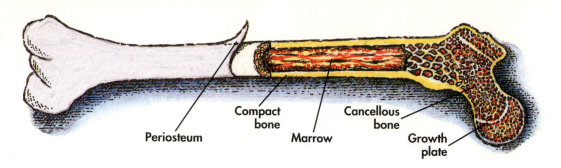

Periosteum   Compact bone   Marrow   Cancellous bone   Growth plate

BODY LANGUAGE

X rays are similar to light rays, but X rays pass through many solid objects. Doctors make X-ray pictures by passing X rays through a patient so that the rays strike a piece of film. Bones block most of the X rays, so they show up as light areas on the pictures.

Inside all bones is a soft, jellylike substance called *marrow* (MAIR oh). Most bones are filled with yellow marrow, which is mainly fat. But certain bones have red marrow inside them. Red marrow is important because it produces the cells that form your blood.

I'm dead, of course. But *your* skeleton—the frame of bones inside you—is very much alive. Your bones still have water and living cells. In fact, throughout your life, your bone tissue is always dissolving and rebuilding itself as blood vessels supply it with minerals.

When you're born, you have about 350 bones and a lot of *cartilage* (KAHR tuh lihj)—a tough, flexible tissue. As you grow, most cartilage turns into bone, except for parts of your nose, ears, and ribcage. Also, many of your

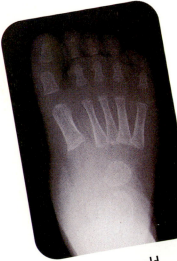

2-1/2-year-old

By comparing these X-ray pictures, you can see how the bones of the foot grow bigger and move closer together.

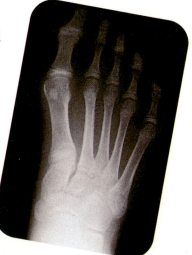

9-year-old

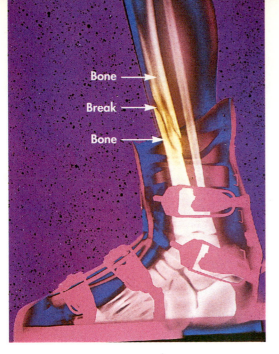

Labels on left image: Bone, Break, Bone

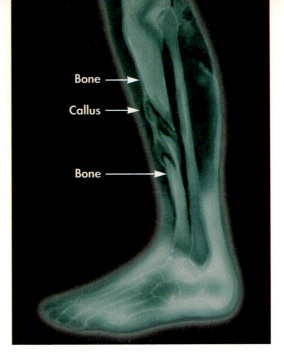

Labels on right image: Bone, Callus, Bone

The X-ray picture, *left,* shows a broken leg in a ski boot. The computer drawing, *right,* shows where a callus of cartilage forms. As the leg heals, the cartilage hardens and turns to bone.

bones fuse, or join—your head wasn't always as hard as a rock. When you're fully grown, you'll have about 200 bones.

The bones of growing children have a *growth plate* (pad of cartilage) near each end. Bones get longer as this cartilage is turned into bone. When a person reaches adulthood, the growth plates stop working and the person stops growing. Bones that are broken grow in a special way in order to heal. At the place of the break, a layer of cartilage and bone called a *callus* forms. The callus surrounds the break and gradually turns to bone.

It's time for me to go back to my closet. Whenever you want me, just knock three times and ask for Mr. Funnybones.

The Bone Song

Y ou may be familiar with the old gospel song "Dry Bones." Here's an updated version. You can sing it two ways: with common names for the bones or scientific names. Look at page 55 if you don't know how to pronounce some of the scientific names.

My toe bones (phalanges) connect up with my foot bones (metatarsals),
My foot bones connect up with my ankle bones (tarsals),
My ankle bones connect up with my shin bone (tibia)–
Let's sing the song of the bones.

Chorus:
Without my bones I can't move around,
Without my bones I fall on the ground,
Without my bones I can't dance or spin–
I'm just a sack of skin.

My shin bone connects up with my knee bone (patella),

My knee bone's connected to my thigh bone (femur),
My thigh bone's connected to my hipbone (ilium)–
Let's sing the song of the bones.

Repeat the chorus

My hipbone's connected to my backbone (vertebral column),
My backbone's connected to my neckbone (cervical vertebrae),
My neckbone's connected to my skull bone–
Let's sing the song of the bones.

Repeat the chorus

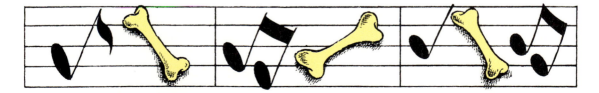

Where the Body Bends

SHOW WILL GO ON FOR BENDER

BEND, OREGON—Brenda the Bendable, a contortionist for Super Circus, was cleared Tuesday of charges that she used illegal means to twist her body into pretzellike knots.

The hinge joint in your knee works like a cabinet hinge, allowing only two-way movement.

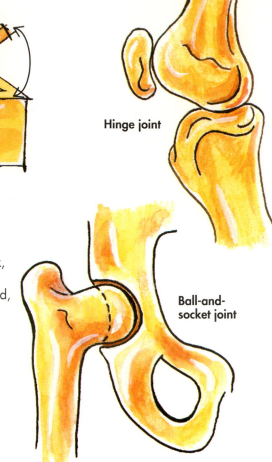

Hinge joint

Ball-and-socket joint

The ball-and-socket joint in your hip works like a joystick, allowing circular movements as well as forward, backward, and sideways movements.

"Most of us have to make do with ordinary joints," said Rubberband Ray of Circus Farkas. "My knees have hinge joints, just like yours. They work like cabinet hinges, allowing only forward and backward movements. But Brenda is so flexible, it seems that she has replaced her hinge joints with ball-and-socket joints."

Most people have ball-and-socket joints only in the hips and shoulders. In these joints, the rounded end of the leg or arm bone fits into a circular hollow in the hip bone or shoulder blade. This joint allows a wide range of motion— forward, backward, sideways, and circular.

"The fixed joints between the bones of my skull are as immovable as anyone else's," Brenda insisted. "And look at the joint between my neck and skull," she said, nodding her head up and down like an ordinary person. "It's the pivot joint I was born with."

"Brenda has all of her original joints," said a spokesperson for the National Union for Contortion and Limberness. "In some places she is *double-jointed*, or able to extend a joint a little farther than normal. But she was born double-jointed, just as many other people were."

Sources close to the circus say that despite claims by jealous competitors, Brenda will go on with the show. Brenda said, "They can bend me but they can't break me."

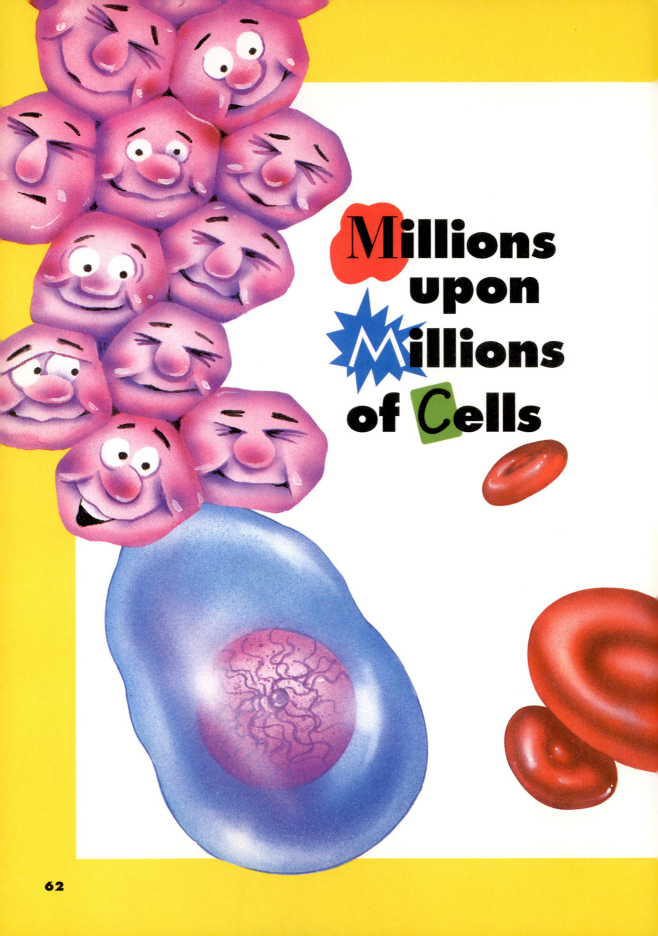

Millions upon Millions of Cells

W

hat do these have in common?

Your neighbor.
The dog your neighbor owns.
The cat that's chased by the dog.
The tree that's climbed by the cat that's
chased by the dog your neighbor owns.

It's not easy to see the answer.

In fact, you'll need a microscope.

That's because the neighbor, the dog,

the cat, and the tree are all made up

of tiny, living cells.

Cell Magic

Welcome to Madame Wizard's World of Wonder, where science and magic meet.

Today, I am going to show you a world so tiny that usually you can only see it through the lens of a microscope. Watch closely as I reveal the magic of cells . . .

What makes cells so magical? Well, without them, life could not exist. Cells are the building blocks of all living things. Just as a snowman is made of tiny snowflakes, all living things are made of tiny cells. Plants are made of cells and so are dogs and insects—and you and me. The human body has over 10 million million cells.

BODY LANGUAGE

In 1665, English scientist Robert Hooke looked at a piece of cork through his microscope. He noticed that the cork was made of "little boxes"–tiny holes surrounded by walls. He called these boxes *cells,* which comes from the Latin word *cella,* meaning "small room."

Red blood cells

Skin cells

As you look at these drawings of cells I have floating before you, you can see that all cells are not alike. For example, cells that make muscles or blood or skin have different shapes. Blood cells are round. Skin cells are almost rectangular. And the cells that make muscles are long and thin.

Cells come in different sizes, too. Some bacteria cells are so small that a row of 50,000 of them would be only 1 inch (2.5 centimeters) long. Most cells in your body are about 1/1,000 inch (.0025 centimeter) wide. It would take hundreds of them to fill the period at the end of this sentence.

The true magic of cells is that they not only make up different parts of living things, but that they also are alive—as alive as you and me. They breathe, take in food, and get rid of wastes. They also grow, *reproduce* (make more of their own kind of cells), and in time, die. And like any

Muscle cells

DNA

Gene

Long, furry tail

Chromosomes

Four legs

Nucleus

Most cats have DNA instructions for a furry tail and four legs. Your DNA has instructions for two legs and two arms.

cell how to use food, how to get rid of wastes, and how to reproduce. Inside the nucleus are structures called chromosomes (KROH muh sohms). *Chromosomes* contain strings of a substance called DNA. *DNA* is like a list of instructions. It tells the cells what they should become. For example, the DNA of a cat's cells includes instructions for a long, furry tail and four legs.

Oh my, I lost track of the time. We had better leave this cell before the membrane decides not to let us out. Please visit again.

BODY BULLETIN

Your longest-lasting cells are nerve cells, which make up much of your brain. But nerve cells are also the only human cells that do not reproduce. So if they die, they are not replaced; they are gone forever.

B O D y science

The Incredible Changing Egg

1. Measure the egg as shown. Then carefully place it in the jar. Pour in enough vinegar to cover the egg. Screw on the lid.

2. Check the egg every day. After three days, carefully remove the egg from the vinegar with a spoon. Measure the egg again. Why did it get bigger?

3. Wash the jar. Then pour in 3 inches (7.5 centimeters) of corn syrup. Carefully place the egg in the jar and screw on the lid. What do you think will happen?

4. Measure the egg after another three days. Why did it shrink?

When you put the egg in vinegar, the vinegar dissolves the shell but leaves the membrane. The membrane is selectively permeable. Water can pass through it, but some other things can't. Water moves through a membrane to the side that has less water. This process is called *osmosis* (ahz MOH sihs). When the egg is in vinegar, water from the vinegar moves into the egg, which contains less water than the vinegar. But when the egg is in syrup, the water moves from the egg into the syrup, which contains less water than the egg. Important fluids move into and out of your body cells in this way–by osmosis.

The Great Grow-Up Show

"What are we going to see?" wondered Sue.

"I'm not sure," said Max, "but Dad said this week's movie would be quite a surprise."

"Here it is," called Dad. "A real family movie—starring me and all of you, growing up."

"What are we looking at now?" asked Sue, pointing at the TV.

"Those are drawings of cells," explained Dad. "We can't have a movie about growing up without them. I, like you and all human beings, began the journey of life as a single cell. But I

Max

didn't stay that small for long, and neither did any of you. You see, that cell divided and became two connected cells. Those two cells became four; those four became eight. This dividing went on until I was a blob of millions of cells."

"But you don't look like a blob," said Sue.

"That's right. At some point in this process of dividing, my cells *specialized,* or became different from one another," explained Dad. "Some formed my legs, some formed my tongue, some formed my ears, and so on."

"Hey! That's me when I was born," yelled Max.

"Right. You were 17 inches (43 centimeters) long and weighed 8 pounds (3.6 kilograms). That's about the size of a sack of potatoes. Of course, you're much bigger now. That's because

BODY LANGUAGE

Mitosis (my TOH sihs) is the process most cells use to divide. Before the start of mitosis, one cell copies all the information in its strands of chromosomes. Then the cell divides into two cells that have chromosomes with exactly the same information.

cells continue to divide after we're born, causing us to grow bigger and bigger. During the first two years of life, a person grows faster than at any other time.

"Look at these pictures. At my first birthday, I was nearly twice as long and heavy as when I was born. It took me about five years to double my size and weight again. By the time I was seven, like you, Sue, I wasn't growing as fast."

"Does that mean this is as tall as I will get?" sighed Sue.

"Not at all. Grandma says I grew almost 2 inches (5 centimeters) taller and about 5 pounds (2.3 kilograms) heavier each year for several years

16 years old

after the first grade. You can see in these photos how much I've grown, just as Max has continued to grow."

"But at this rate, Dad, I'll never be tall enough to play basketball," said Max.

"Just wait until you reach puberty (PYOO buhr tee), Max. *Puberty* is a time of life when the body changes a lot, and the cells divide like crazy. In fact, the body can grow quite a bit in a short time. Such growth spurts happen at slightly different times for different people. During my growth spurt, I grew a little more than 3 inches (7.6 centimeters) a year," Dad said. "But after puberty, my body did not grow much more.

"Look at these videos of our family picnics. See how you kids all grew taller each year, but

BODY BULLETIN

As you grow bigger, different parts of your body grow bigger at different speeds. As a baby, you have a large head and body compared with your short arms and legs. Over the years, your head grows only a little bit, your body slightly faster, your arms even faster, and your legs fastest of all.

73

10/4/94 12:26 p.m.

6/13/90 11:35 a.m.

Mom and I stayed the same height? That happened because between the ages of twenty and fifty, the body doesn't normally grow taller. During this time, however, the cells are still very busy. They continue to die off and be replaced with new ones.

"At about age sixty, Grandpa's age, cells don't divide and replace themselves as quickly and effectively. As a result, the body may get sick more easily."

"Is that why Grandpa's broken arm took longer to heal than mine?" asked Sue.

"Right," Dad replied. "This change in the production of the cells is also why it's so important to take care of yourself and your cells while you're growing up.

"That's it for this movie. Let's go take some more videos of us growing up together."

R UDOLF V IRCHOW

The idea that all living things are made of cells and that all of life's activities take place in these cells is called the *cell theory.* Scientists are well aware of this idea today. But in the 1800's, scientists knew little about cells and did not realize the importance of cells to all life. One of a number of people who helped develop the cell theory was Rudolf Virchow (1821-1900), a German medical scientist and political official.

After performing years of research and studying the work of other scientists, Rudolf became convinced that the tissues of all living things were made of cells. He later showed that the effects of diseases could be detected by observing cells through a microscope. In time, his ideas about cells and disease greatly changed medicine. Today, Rudolf is known as the "father of pathology" (puh THAHL uh jee). *Pathology*

is the study of diseases and their effects on body tissues and organs.

During his career, Rudolf studied and wrote about the effects of different diseases on body tissues. In 1845, he described *leukemia* (loo KEE mee uh), a kind of cancer. Rudolf was also one of the first scientists to describe the process of *inflammation.* Have you ever noticed that after you cut yourself the skin cells around the cut become red and swollen? That is inflammation at work, fighting off infection.

Rudolf later went into politics. As an elected official, he worked hard to protect the health of the public. For instance, he became interested in how animal *parasites* (PAIR uh syts), tiny living things that live on animals, cause disease in humans. Some of these parasites found their way into humans through the meat that humans ate. As a result of the efforts of Rudolf and others, most countries now have guidelines for producing meat that is safe for you to eat.

Rudolf Virchow, *below center with beard and glasses,* is shown observing an operation in 1900.

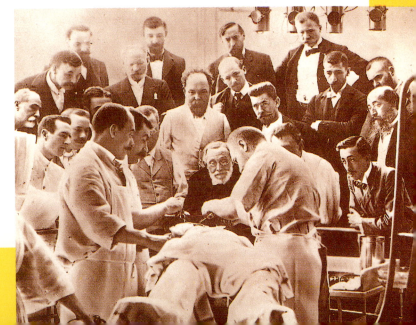

Your Cell and Tissue Teams

We all know that teamwork is the name of the game, right? When people work together, things tend to run smoothly. Well, the same is also true for cells.

At some point when a cell divides, it becomes a specialist. That is, it becomes a certain kind of cell that performs a specific task. For example, some cells become muscle cells, some become skin cells, and some become blood cells. Then cells of the same kind gather together, or team up, to form *tissues*. For example, teams of

Your cells become specialists to make up different kinds of tissue.

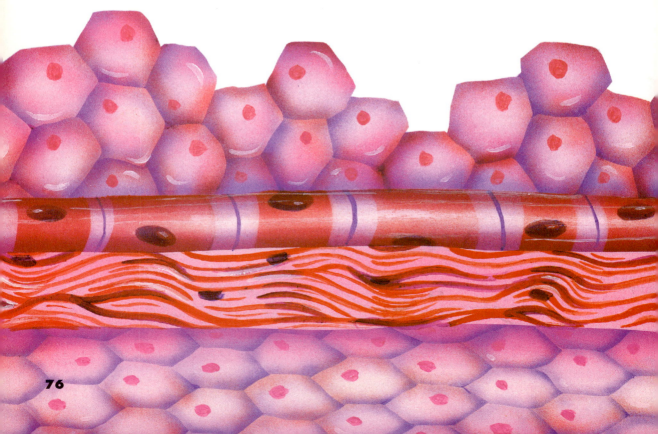

muscle cells form muscles. The cells work together so that muscles can do their job.

The human body is made up of four main kinds of tissues: epithelial (EH puh THEE lee uhl) tissue, muscle tissue, connective tissue, and nerve tissue. Let's meet the teams of cells that make these tissues.

"To be an epithelial cell, you have to like working very close to your teammates. We're packed into epithelial tissue like sardines. This tissue forms part of the skin and the inside lining of body openings such as the nose, mouth, and throat. It helps prevent harmful substances from entering the body. Epithelial tissue also helps line body parts, such as your heart and stomach."

Epithelial cells

Epithelial tissue

Muscle tissue

Connective tissue

Epithelial tissue

Blood (a special kind of tissue)

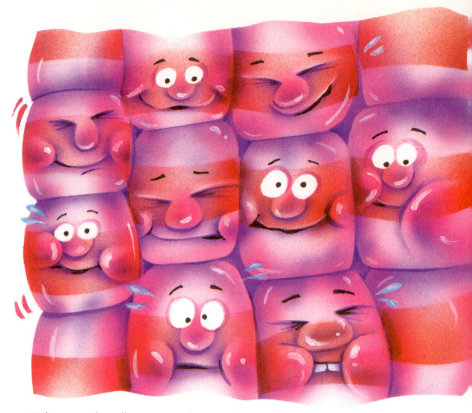

When muscle cells contract, the muscle tissue gets shorter and thicker.

When muscle cells relax, the muscle tissue can get longer and thinner.

"Pardon us if we keep moving while we talk. You caught us in the middle of our workout. We're the cells that form the body's muscles. We *contract* (get shorter) and relax to allow muscle tissue to move the parts of the body. We also allow muscles to help move substances through the body."

"Even though we've just met, we feel 'connected' to you already. We're the cells that make connective tissue. Between each and every one of us are fibers and a jellylike substance. Because we are strong and elastic, connective tissue does many things for the body. For example, it joins parts of the body.

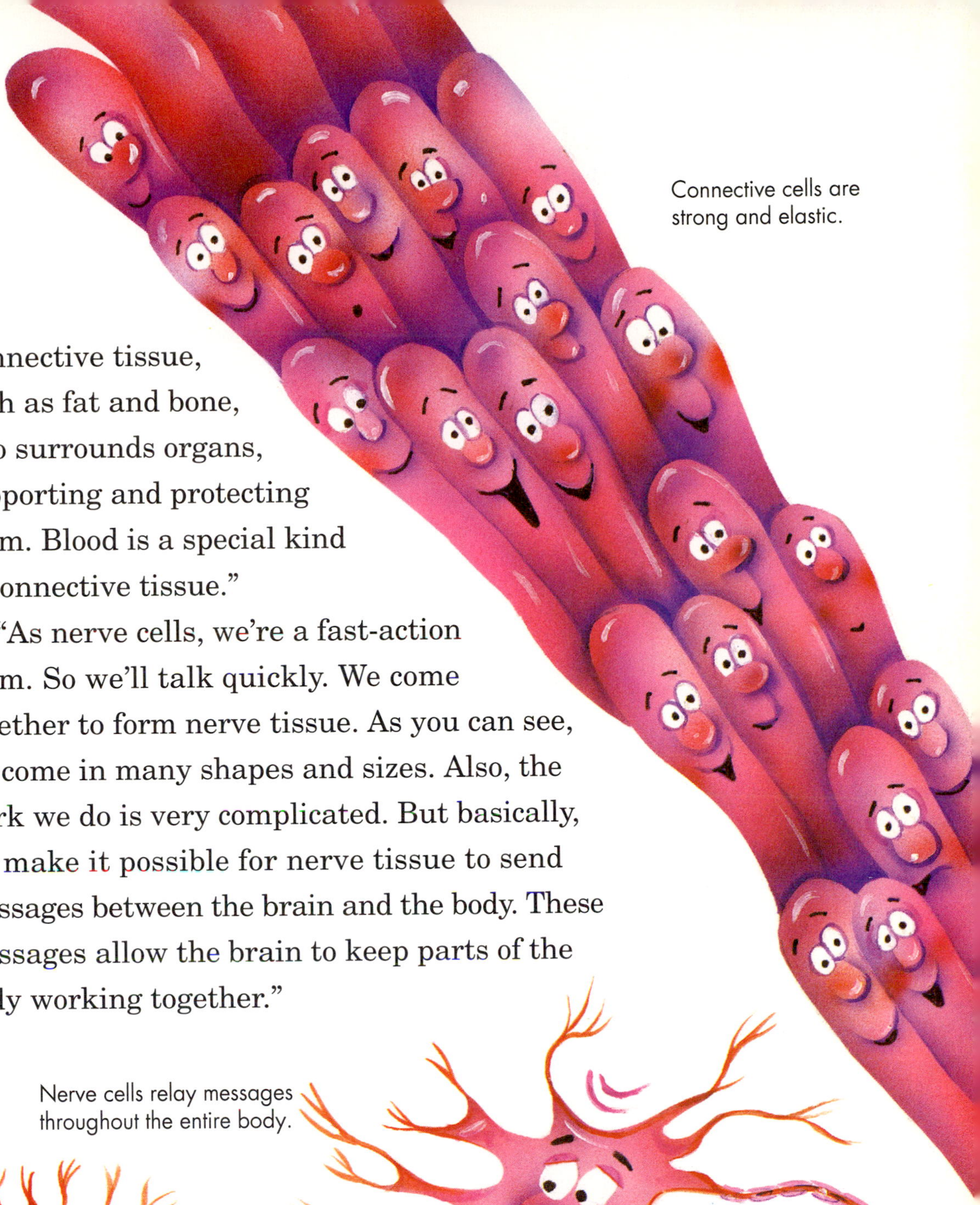

Connective cells are strong and elastic.

Connective tissue,
such as fat and bone,
also surrounds organs,
supporting and protecting
them. Blood is a special kind
of connective tissue."

"As nerve cells, we're a fast-action
team. So we'll talk quickly. We come
together to form nerve tissue. As you can see,
we come in many shapes and sizes. Also, the
work we do is very complicated. But basically,
we make it possible for nerve tissue to send
messages between the brain and the body. These
messages allow the brain to keep parts of the
body working together."

Nerve cells relay messages
throughout the entire body.

Just as groups of cells make tissues, different tissues team up to make organs. An *organ* is made of two or more kinds of tissues joined to do a certain job. The heart, for example, is made of mostly muscle tissue and epithelial tissue.

But that's still not the end of your body's teamwork. Organs form teams of their own to make body systems. Each system has a role in keeping the body healthy. For example, your heart, blood vessels, and blood are some of the players that make up your *circulatory* (SUHR kyuh luh TOHR ee) system, which moves blood throughout your body.

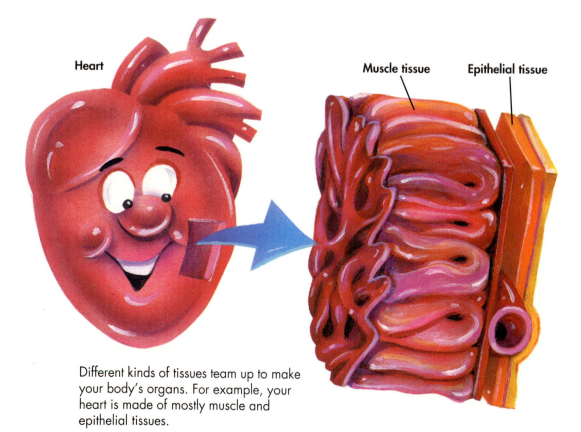

Heart

Muscle tissue

Epithelial tissue

Different kinds of tissues team up to make your body's organs. For example, your heart is made of mostly muscle and epithelial tissues.

How Does a Nose Know Where to Grow?

This cell, magnified thousands of times its size, is splitting into two cells. Each will specialize depending on which of its genes get "turned on."

A nose can be big or small, long or short, bumpy or smooth. But there's one thing about a nose that's certain: It knows just where to grow. So do the feet, the arms, the heart, and every other part of the body.

How do all the parts of the body fall into the right place? The answer lies in DNA, the body's instructions.

When cells divide, they pass along an exact copy of all their chromosomes to the newly formed cells. Because each new cell has the same chromosomes, each also has the same DNA. So it seems as if all these new cells would be exactly the same. But that's not how it works.

At some point, cells begin to specialize. Some become muscle cells, and some become other kinds, such as blood cells and nerve cells.

But if all cells have the same DNA, how do some cells become muscle cells while other cells become nerve, blood, or bone cells?

Each string of DNA is lined with genes. Scientists believe that different combinations of these genes get "turned on," or become active, in different kinds of cells. When certain genes are "turned on," the cell becomes a muscle cell. Skin cells and nerve cells form when other gene combinations are turned on in other cells.

Scientists still aren't sure what turns on certain genes in some cells and other genes in other cells. But you see, a nose knows where to grow because its DNA tells it so.

Touring Your Lungs and Heart

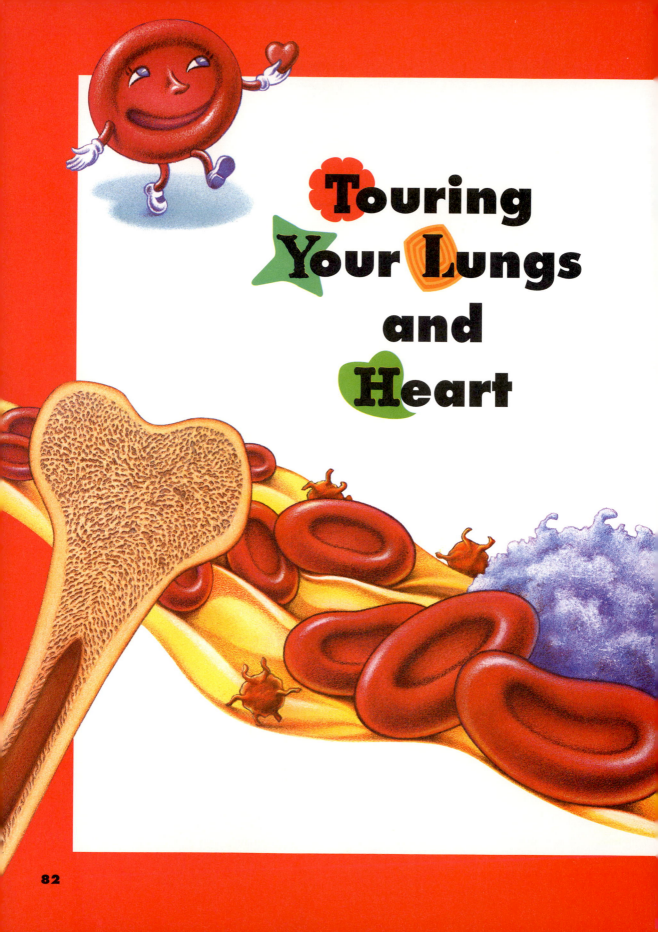

Round and round and round they go—oxygen and wastes, you know. Your lungs bring oxygen into the body, and they send wastes out. Your heart acts as the main pump, moving fresh oxygen to your cells and driving wastes away.

Your Breathing Machine

Congratulations! You are the proud owner of a set of lungs. With proper care, they will provide you with a lifetime of healthy breathing.

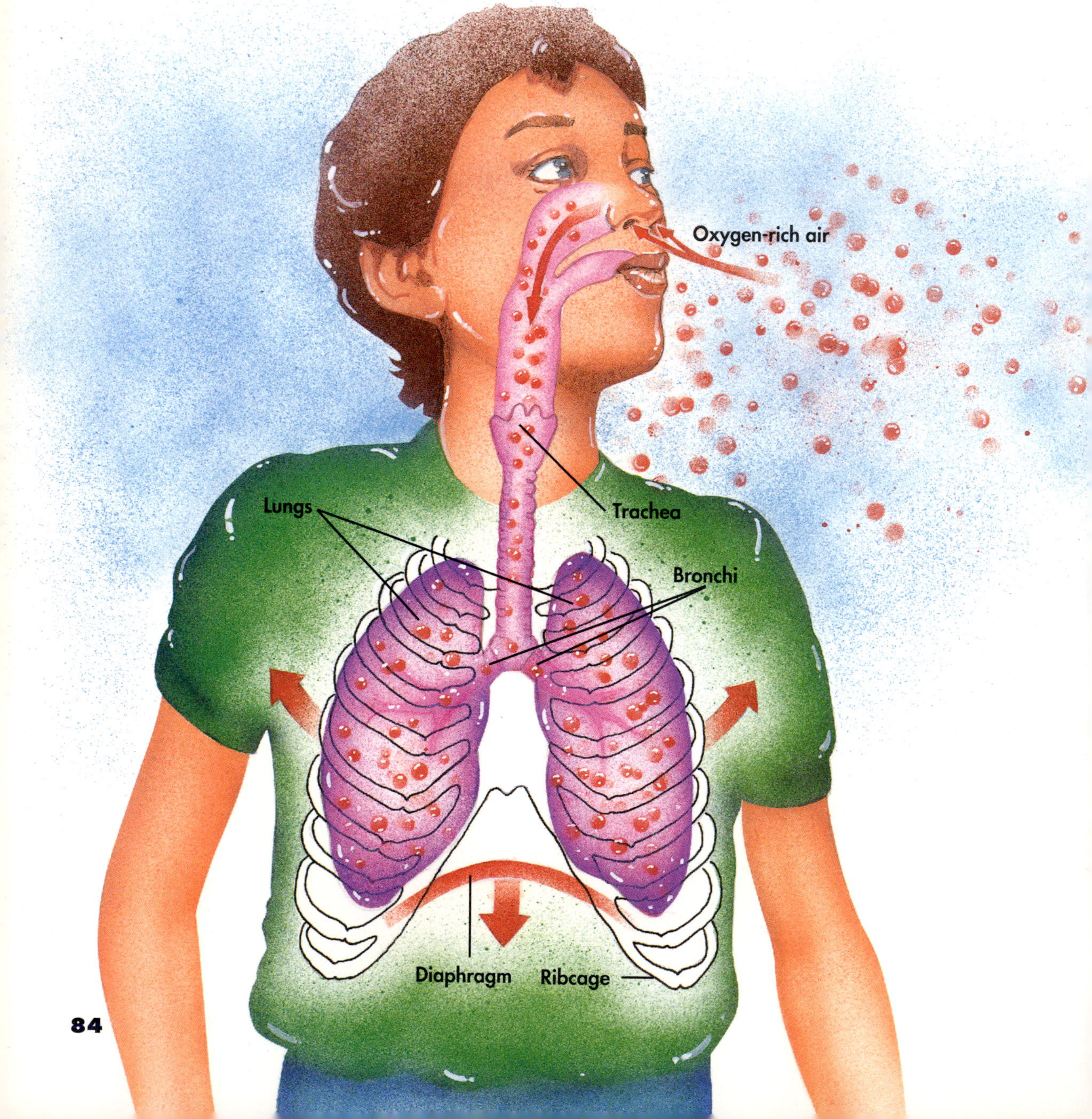

Oxygen-rich air

Lungs

Trachea

Bronchi

Diaphragm   Ribcage

SETUP

Your lungs have come fully assembled and fitted into your body. They are spongy and elastic— prepared to take in even your deepest breaths. Your lungs fill most of the center of your chest cavity, safely surrounded by your ribcage and your spine. The left lung is slightly smaller than the right to allow room for your heart.

From above, your windpipe, or trachea (TRAY kee uh), brings in air from your nose and mouth. Two smaller tubes called the bronchi (BRAHNG ky) bring the air from the trachea

to the lungs. Below your lungs is the diaphragm (DY uh fram), a large muscle on the bottom of your chest cavity. If you are breathing easily, you can be assured that your lungs are set up properly.

PARTS

The bronchi lead from the trachea to the lungs. Tiny hairlike structures called *cilia* (SIHL ee uh) line these airways to sweep out harmful invaders. The bronchi branch into smaller and smaller bronchi, and eventually into very tiny tubes called *bronchioles* (BRAHNG kee ohlz). The bronchioles divide, too. The tiniest

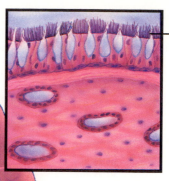

Cilia

Bronchioles

Self-Cleaning

Tiny, hairlike cilia line your trachea and bronchi. The cilia help sweep out harmful invaders before they get to your lungs.

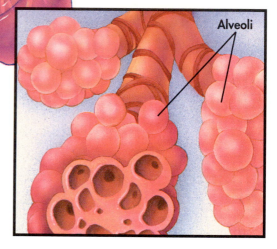

Alveoli

Maximum Capacity

Your smallest bronchioles lead to tiny air sacs called alveoli. These sacs are coated with mucus and surfactant, materials that moisten the sacs and help them expand and hold air when you inhale.

bronchioles lead to passages lined with tiny air sacs called *alveoli* (al VEE uh ly). Each lung contains about 300 million alveoli. *Mucus* (MYOO kuhs) keeps the sacs moist. Fatty materials called *surfactants* (suhr FAK tuhnts) coat the inside of the alveoli to help them expand and stay filled with air. Outside the alveoli are the *pulmonary capillaries,* extremely small blood vessels.

HOW YOUR LUNGS WORK

Your lungs bring oxygen into your body and take carbon dioxide out with the help of surrounding nerve and muscle cells. Special nerve cells in your brain detect when there is too much carbon dioxide and not enough oxygen in your body. When the nerves signal, the muscles in your chest cavity and the diaphragm contract. They pull outward, upward, and downward to make the space inside your chest larger. As you inhale, your lungs expand and draw in oxygen-rich air through your nose or mouth. When you exhale, the muscles relax, pushing out carbon dioxide your lungs have received from your blood cells.

Your diaphragm and chest cavity contract when you inhale, *below left*. They relax when you exhale, *below right*.

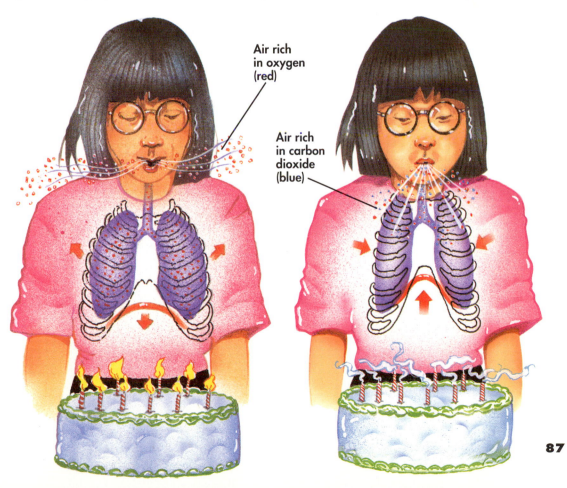

Air rich in oxygen (red)

Air rich in carbon dioxide (blue)

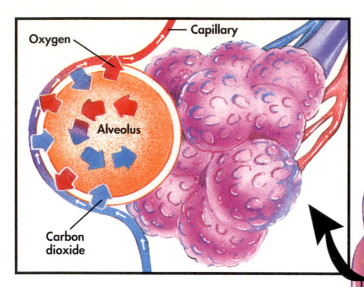

Oxygen

Capillary

Alveolus

Carbon dioxide

The most important work of the lungs takes place in the alveoli. As blood passes over an alveolus sac (see the white arrows), it drops off carbon dioxide and picks up oxygen. The arrows inside the sac show the path of air you inhale. Air enters the sac rich in oxygen. It gives its oxygen to the blood in exchange for harmful carbon dioxide, then leaves the sac—and eventually your body.

The actual exchange of gases occurs in the alveoli. The alveoli trade their oxygen for the carbon dioxide in the blood in the pulmonary capillaries. After the blood picks up the oxygen, it returns to the heart. The heart then pumps the oxygen-rich blood to the rest of the body.

CARE AND MAINTENANCE

Avoid cigarette smoke and other pollutants. These substances can block air tubes and damage the walls of your alveoli so that oxygen and carbon dioxide can't pass through. If your lungs function poorly, see your doctor for repairs. And remember, for best results, give your lungs deep breaths of fresh air.

What Caused That Bloody Nose?

The mucous membranes that collect dust in the nose are very delicate. They are sensitive to cold and to dry air. They also contain many small blood vessels that are very close to the surface of the membranes inside the nostrils.

Sometimes the mucous membranes become too dry. They often become dry in winter, or as a result of a cold. They also dry out easily in people with a *deviated septum* (DEE vee ayt ed SEHP tuhm)– a crooked wall between the nostrils. When the mucous membranes are too dry, a small scratch or a slight knock can be enough to break

blood vessels and cause a nosebleed.

To stop a nosebleed caused by irritation, sit down, lean forward, and pinch your nostrils together for about ten minutes. Or, insert a small, clean piece of gauze partway into each nostril and apply pressure.

Severe nosebleeds may be a sign of a serious illness or a broken blood vessel farther back in the nose. They can be dangerous. If you or someone you know has a heavy nosebleed, you might need to call a doctor. Ask an adult for help at once.

One way to stop a nosebleed is to sit down, lean forward, and pinch your nostrils closed for about ten minutes.

Air Alert!

Nancy Nose

Healthy Harold

"Healthy Harold here, with the fresh air news. Each day, you and I spend all day breathing. But with all the smoke, dust, and air pollution around, I can't help but wonder, 'Isn't breathing bad for you and me?' Let's ask the experts.

"Nancy Nose, I see that almost every bit of air that goes into the lungs goes through you. How do you keep breathing?"

NN: "Well, Harold, I do see a lot of grime and dirt, but I have teams of *mucus* and *cilia* that help keep the body safe. They work to keep out bad materials, such as dust, pollutants, bacteria, and viruses. The sticky mucus traps most intruders. Then the hairlike cilia sweep them down to the throat to be coughed up or swallowed. In fact, the mucus also warms and moistens cold, dry air before it gets to the lungs."

Tom Trachea

Marla Mouth

Eddie Epiglottis

MM: "I'm Marla Mouth, and I'd like to get a word in. When Nancy gets stuffy or tickled by smoke or dirt, I breathe in air so she can sneeze out germs and dust. I move air fast, but I don't have the mucus or cilia Nancy has to clean, moisten, and warm the air."

TT: "Don't forget, all the air that Nancy and Marla bring in goes through me, Tom Trachea, before it gets to the lungs. Like Nancy, I have mucus and cilia to protect the lungs. They trap most dust and other materials and sweep them up to the throat where they can be coughed up or swallowed."

Trachea
Esophagus
Lungs
Epiglottis (closed)

EE: "I'm Eddie Epiglottis, Tom Trachea's bodyguard. Sometimes Marla has really got her mouth full with lunch or dinner. That's when I come in. I help make sure that Tom gets only air, no pizza or apples. When Marla works with food, I close over Tom to protect him. If food gets past me, the nerves signal us to cough it up."

HH: "So, folks, breathing is pretty safe. Nancy, Marla, Tom, Eddie, thanks for being with us."

Voices are like fingerprints—
no two are exactly alike.

Top View of Voice Box

Epiglottis

Vocal cords

Trachea

You may not belong to an orchestra or band, but whenever you speak, you play a one-of-a-kind musical instrument. The instrument is your *larynx* (LAIR ingks), or voice box. You've been practicing on it since the day you were born.

Your larynx sits at the top of your windpipe, or trachea. Inside are two folds of elastic tissue, one stretched along each side– just like the strings of a piano, guitar, violin, harp, or cello. These folds are called *vocal cords*.

When you hum, or shout, or speak, or sing, you pass air through your larynx. As the air passes through, your vocal cords vibrate and make sounds that echo through your chest, mouth, and nose.

People with shorter, thinner vocal cords usually produce higher-pitched sounds. People who have longer, thicker vocal cords usually produce deeper sounds.

However, there are many ways you can vary the sounds you make. You can make higher sounds by tensing your vocal cords or lower sounds by relaxing them. You can also create a variety of sounds by moving your mouth, lips, teeth, and tongue. Try it and hear.

Perhaps the most interesting thing about your voice is you. Since no two people have the same vocal cords, chest, mouth, or nose, no two voices are exactly alike. In fact, scientists say that just as each person has a unique set of fingerprints, so does each person have a unique voice.

93

The Heart of the Matter

People often say, "Have a heart" or "I'm brokenhearted." But everyone has a heart, and hearts don't break. I'm a blood cell, and I've seen hearts plenty of times in my life. Your heart is small and muscular, about the size of your fist. It keeps blood cells like me pumping through your body. Your heart sits between your lungs, near the middle of your chest cavity. A tough, thin sac protects it from rubbing against the chest cavity and the lungs.

Your heart is made mostly of muscular walls. Special cells in the heart control the heartbeat. The cells send electrical signals through the heart, causing it to contract and relax. As it contracts and relaxes, blood vessels bring blood into—and out of—the four heart chambers. The two chambers closest to your right hand receive blood from the body and pump it to the lungs to get oxygen. The two chambers closest to your left hand pump blood from the lungs to other parts of your body. Valves between the chambers help keep the blood going one way.

If you put your hand on your chest, you'll feel your heart beating. It keeps beating whether you're eating, sleeping, or playing. Well, I've got to get circulating. Good bye!

BODY BULLETIN

The heartbeat your doctor listens to is really the sound produced by the closing of the heart's valves. With every beat, your heart pushes only about three tablespoons of blood through your body–so you can see why it needs to keep pumping all day long.

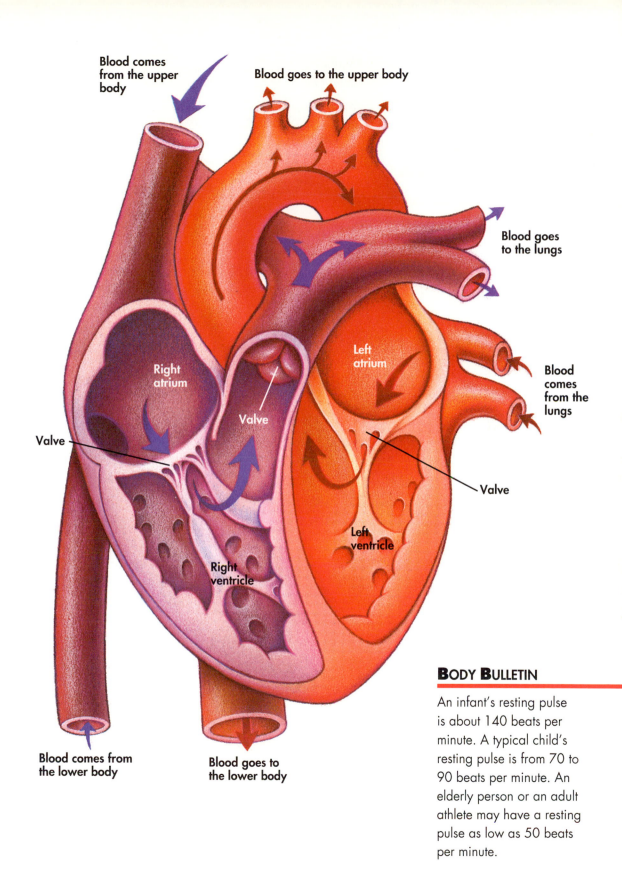

Blood comes from the upper body

Blood goes to the upper body

Blood goes to the lungs

Blood comes from the lungs

Right atrium

Valve

Left atrium

Valve

Valve

Left ventricle

Right ventricle

Blood comes from the lower body

Blood goes to the lower body

BODY BULLETIN

An infant's resting pulse is about 140 beats per minute. A typical child's resting pulse is from 70 to 90 beats per minute. An elderly person or an adult athlete may have a resting pulse as low as 50 beats per minute.

Putting Your Pulse on Paper

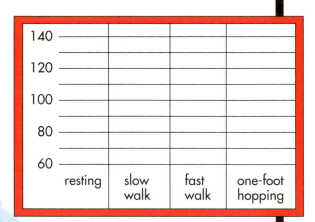

	resting	slow walk	fast walk	one-foot hopping
140				
120				
100				
80				
60				

How hard does your heart work? Find out by counting your pulse.

1. Make a grid like the one shown above. List heart rates in the column at the left, from 140 at the top to 60 at the bottom. List different activities in the row across the bottom, beginning with "resting." Predict which activities will make your heart beat fastest and slowest.

2. Sit quietly for a few minutes. Then, for 15 seconds, count your *pulse*– the number of "thumps" you feel with your finger on the artery in your wrist. Or, place a toothpick in a dab of clay and put it on your wrist. Count the number of times the toothpick moves in 15 seconds. Multiply your number by 4 to find the beats in 1 minute.

3. Mark the final number on the chart as your resting heart rate.

4. Now try each of the activities you listed. Do one for a minute. Take your pulse and record it on the chart immediately after you stop. Rest for a few minutes, then do another activity. Which produces the highest pulse rate?

A Closer Look at Blood

Things aren't always what they seem—especially when it comes to blood! If someone asked you to describe your blood, you would probably say it is a red liquid. In a way, you'd be right. It *looks* like a red liquid. But it's actually much more. Let's take a closer look.

Your blood is mainly made up of a yellowish clear liquid called *plasma* (PLAZ muh) and blood cells. The blood cells swim in the river of plasma, which makes up more than 55 percent of your blood. Plasma is mostly water, but it also consists of hundreds of other substances—such as nutrients, hormones, and waste. It carries these substances throughout your bloodstream.

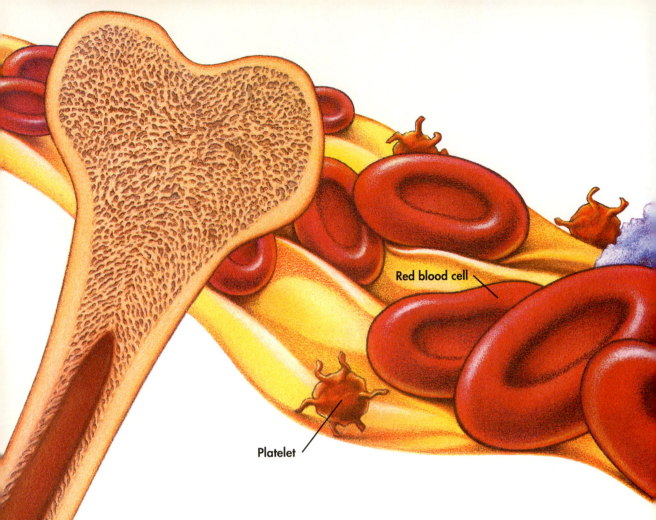

Red blood cell

Platelet

Most blood cells are produced in bone marrow. There are red blood cells, white blood cells, and platelets.

An average person's blood contains about 25 trillion red blood cells. These saucer-shaped cells carry oxygen through the body and help get rid of carbon dioxide. Even though these are called red blood cells, they can be dull looking or even bluish when they are low on oxygen. Red blood cells live in the body about 120 days. In one second, the body destroys about 2 million of them—and builds as many new ones.

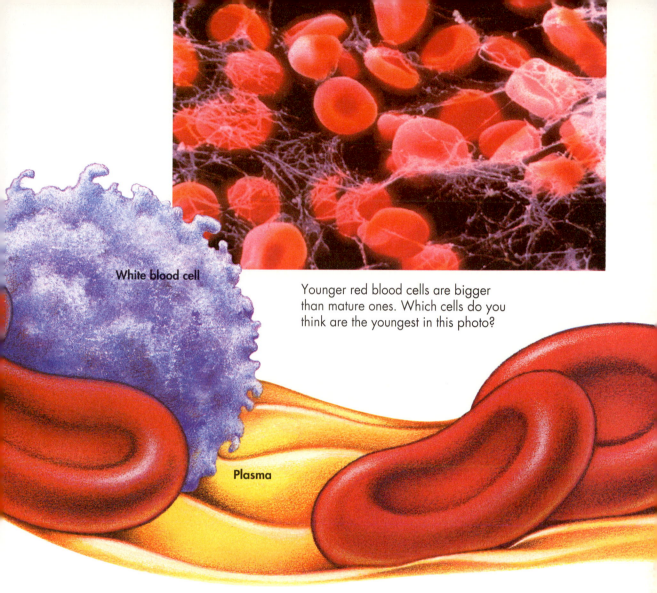

White blood cell

Younger red blood cells are bigger than mature ones. Which cells do you think are the youngest in this photo?

Plasma

White blood cells help protect the body against infections and diseases. These cells come in many sizes and shapes. Some kinds are larger than red blood cells. An average person's blood contains about 25 billion white blood cells.

Platelets (PLAYT lihts) help your cuts and scrapes heal. They are the smallest blood cells— only half the size of red ones. Platelets live only about ten days. The average person has about 1,250 billion platelets.

BODY BULLETIN

Doctors often categorize a person's blood into one of these types: A, B, AB, or O. For blood transfusions, doctors need to know the patient's blood type. Giving a patient the wrong type would cause the patient's blood to clot too much.

Some**BODY** you should know

CHARLES DREW

Charles Drew (1904-1950) was at Amherst College when he decided to become a doctor. While he was in the hospital with a football injury, his doctor took him to visit a fan. Charles learned that the boy had almost died from lack of blood. Blood banks were not common then, and the hospital's blood supply was low. Blood can be stored for only a week before red blood cells break down.

After college, Charles went to McGill University in Montreal, Canada. At a hospital there, he again saw a patient suffer from a blood shortage. This time, he offered his own blood, and the patient was saved.

Charles became an excellent surgeon. He taught at Howard University and Columbia University. He also began a blood bank.

Charles conducted research with the help of his wife, Lenore. He became determined to find a way to preserve and store blood. He knew it was more than 55 percent plasma, which does not break down as quickly as red blood cells. He also realized that plasma could match any blood type, because it does not contain red blood cells. He decided to find out if plasma could be an emergency stand-in for whole blood.

During World War II, Charles and others worked on a committee that sent plasma to British and American soldiers who desperately needed blood. It worked! He and his fellow researchers saved thousands of lives.

When the United States War Department ordered that blood be separated by race, Charles refused. He resigned from the committee. After the war, Charles continued his work as a doctor, researcher, and teacher.

Charles Drew in 1947

Exploring Your Circulatory System

Hello! Stanley Livingcell here! I'm so glad you can join me as I go rafting through the body on a red blood cell.

The red blood cell that I have chosen is fairly young. It has made only 40,000 trips to and from the heart, and still has about 120,000 trips left in its career.

After that, it will probably get recycled in the liver and spleen. Ah, there's my cell! It's looking quite dull because it's low on oxygen. That means we'll have to raft through the veins to the heart so the blood cell can get to the lungs and pick up some.

Here we go, into the right atrium of the heart and then into the right ventricle. The right ventricle pushes us to the lungs so the cell can pick up oxygen and drop off carbon dioxide. The main job of red blood cells is to deliver oxygen to other cells and pick up their waste.

BODY LANGUAGE

The word *circulation* comes from a word meaning "circle." Your heart and blood vessels are called your *circulatory system* because they help blood circle through your body.

We have a short visit in the left atrium. Now the valve is opening to let us into the left ventricle. Whoosh! We are being pumped into the artery called the aorta (ay AWR tuh). These large arteries near the heart can carry a lot of traffic. As we float in the clear, swiftly moving plasma, watch all the action that goes on in this vast trade route called the circulatory system. See how cleverly our red blood cell has been trading with other body cells along the way? It's giving them oxygen and taking carbon dioxide in return.

We are lucky to be traveling just after dinner. The heart beats rather fast after meals. It rushes blood down to help the stomach and small intestine digest food. The plasma in the blood absorbs waste materials and nutrients from the food, and the blood delivers the nutrients to other body cells along the route.

Now we're being pumped through the liver. The liver helps purify blood by breaking down or filtering poisons and wastes the blood has picked up from the body. As we pass through the kidneys, more wastes are taken out of the blood for disposal.

Liver

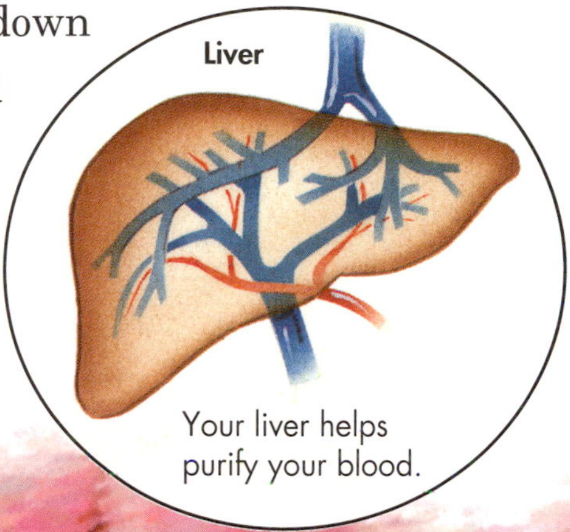

Your liver helps purify your blood.

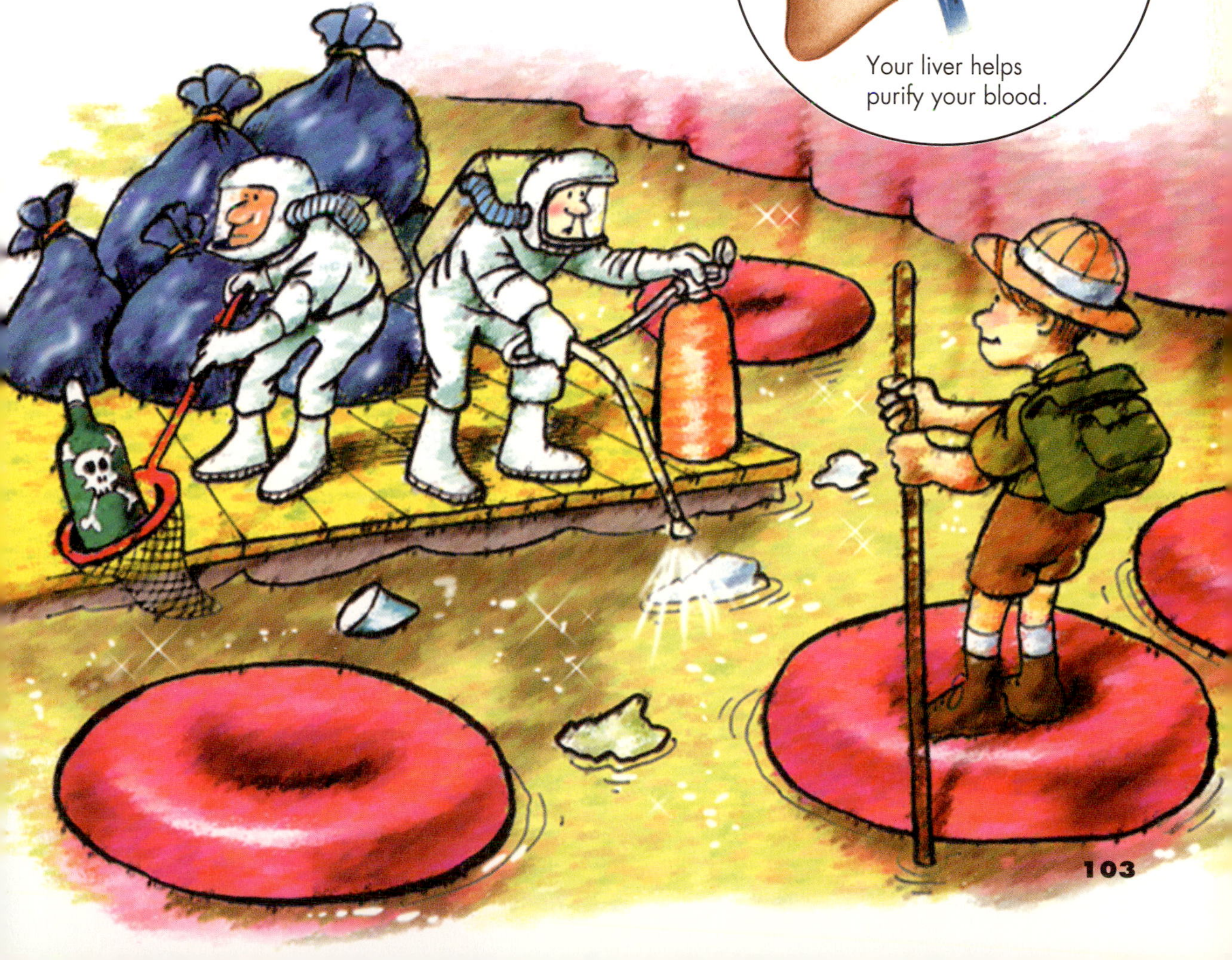

103

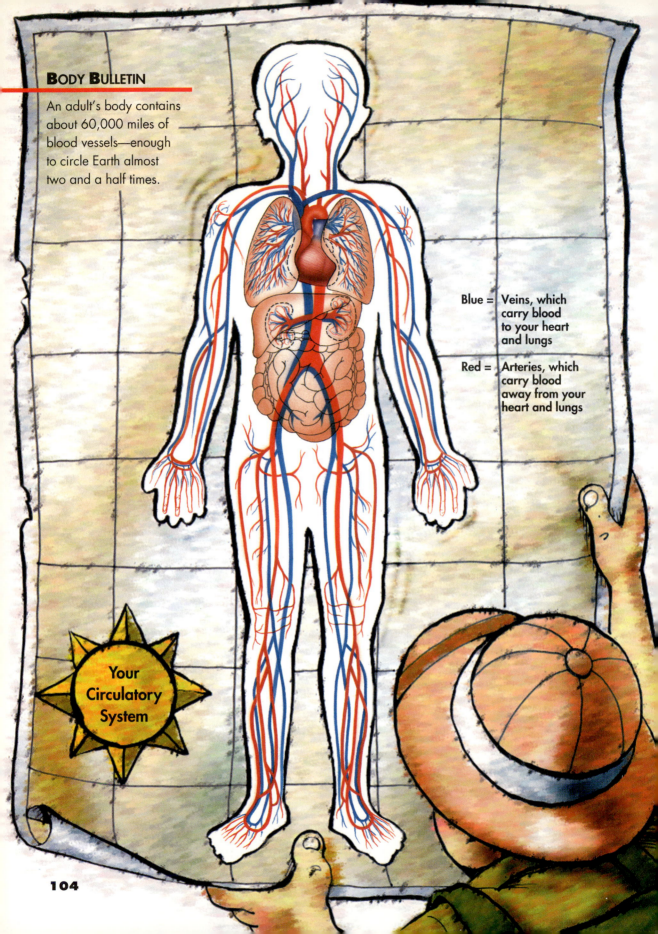

BODY BULLETIN

An adult's body contains about 60,000 miles of blood vessels—enough to circle Earth almost two and a half times.

Blue = Veins, which carry blood to your heart and lungs

Red = Arteries, which carry blood away from your heart and lungs

Your Circulatory System

We sure have traveled far from the heart and lungs. You can tell because the blood vessels are getting narrower and the blood current is slowing. The smallest vessels are the capillaries. There are so many of these! Will we be stranded here, low on oxygen, in the capillary wilderness of the big toe?

Capillaries connect your smallest arteries with your smallest veins.

Not at all! Even here, we are in touch with the beat of the heart. The capillaries contract and push the cells single file through to another capillary—and then on to the veins! The veins lead us back to the heart. From there, the red blood cell will go to the lungs, exchange the carbon dioxide for oxygen, then go back to the heart and begin circulating through the arteries again.

Let's hop off here, where we started. It's been a thrilling experience. Thanks for coming along.

BODY BULLETIN

When a blood vessel breaks, it bleeds. But if the skin doesn't break, the bleeding stays under the skin and appears as a bruise.

An adhesive bandage helps keep a cut clean while the body heals itself.

Chances are you've scraped, bumped, and scratched yourself dozens of times. Yet you're none the worse for wear. That's because your blood has more than a billion platelets that help stop bleeding.

Platelets are the heroes of blood clotting. When you cut yourself, muscles around your blood vessels contract to slow the bleeding. At the same time, platelets come to the surface. They plug up the cut and the area around it. Then they send messages to the body to form clotting proteins called *fibrin* (FY brihn).

Fibrin forms a criss-crossed net across the cut that pulls tighter as it dries. The clot at the surface becomes a scab, which protects the cut as it heals.

For most people, clots help heal cuts and scrapes.

However, some people have a condition called *hemophilia* (HEE muh FIHL ee uh). These people have to be careful not to hurt themselves too much because their blood does not clot properly. Other people with partially clogged arteries have to be careful that clotting does not completely block their blood circulation.

You can help keep your arteries clear for platelets to do their job by exercising daily and eating foods that are low in fat.

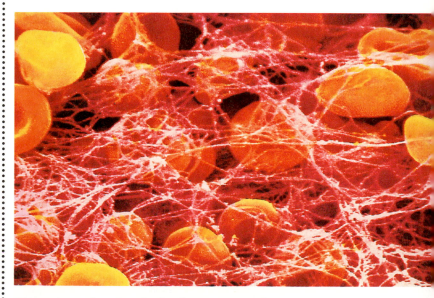

Fibrin, shown here hundreds of times its actual size, forms a net to help blood clot.

Fighters For Your Life

There are 25 billion stories in the human body—one for every white blood cell. You say you want to join my unit? First, let me tell you how we operate.

We white blood cells are proud to be part of the immune system security team. Most of us are colorless, but we come in a variety of sizes and shapes. We *leukocytes* (LOO kuh syts), or white blood cells, may be known as "killer cells," but we're just doing our job. We are sworn to serve and protect the body from bacteria, viruses, and abnormal cells.

Some white blood cells come from the spleen or bone marrow. They eat up germs that come their way. It's important work, but it's not for me. I'm one of the *lymphocytes* (LIHM fuh syts), probably the most powerful group of white blood

BODY BULLETIN

Immunization shots contain a small dose of the virus or bacteria that cause the disease you are trying to *avoid*. The small, weak dose alerts your immune system to make the antibodies that will protect you against the disease.

107

1 A leukocyte, background, approaches a cluster of bacteria.

cells on the force. We come from the *lymph nodes,* a type of body tissue that helps the immune security system.

The whole body is my beat. I trail cells endlessly, looking for viruses, bacteria, and abnormal cells. Diseases drive me crazy. When I spot one, I run to the nearest lymph node and spread the word about what I've found. Other white blood cells called *neutrophils* (NOO truh fihlz) attack the harmful organism first.

2 The leukocyte surrounds the bacteria.

Sometimes, if the infection is not so bad, the advance squad of neutrophils takes care of the disturbance. They actually eat abnormal cells—if they don't get eaten first. Most of the time, though, they need me to finish the job. It's a tough business, but it's better than letting disease run wild. I get busy building *antibodies,* special proteins that will help destroy the harmful organism, as fast as I can. When I get to the scene, I surround the enemy and disable it. Often, I kill it.

In my short life, I've seen some white blood cells stay on the force for only a few hours. Others battle for many years. I've seen our force fight the gangs known as flu, strep, chickenpox, and countless petty colds. I also have been trained to search out and destroy rubella, diphtheria, measles, mumps, and *pertussis*—alias whooping cough. The force has helped wipe out smallpox, and we're putting the pressure on polio, too. None of those measly bugs last very long around here!

Oh no, gotta go! A new virus is trying to invade the sinuses.

3 The leukocyte swallows and destroys the bacteria.

BODY LANGUAGE

People with **allergies** are unusually sensitive to a particular substance or substances. Their antibodies attack these substances–such as dust or certain foods–which are often harmless to many other people.

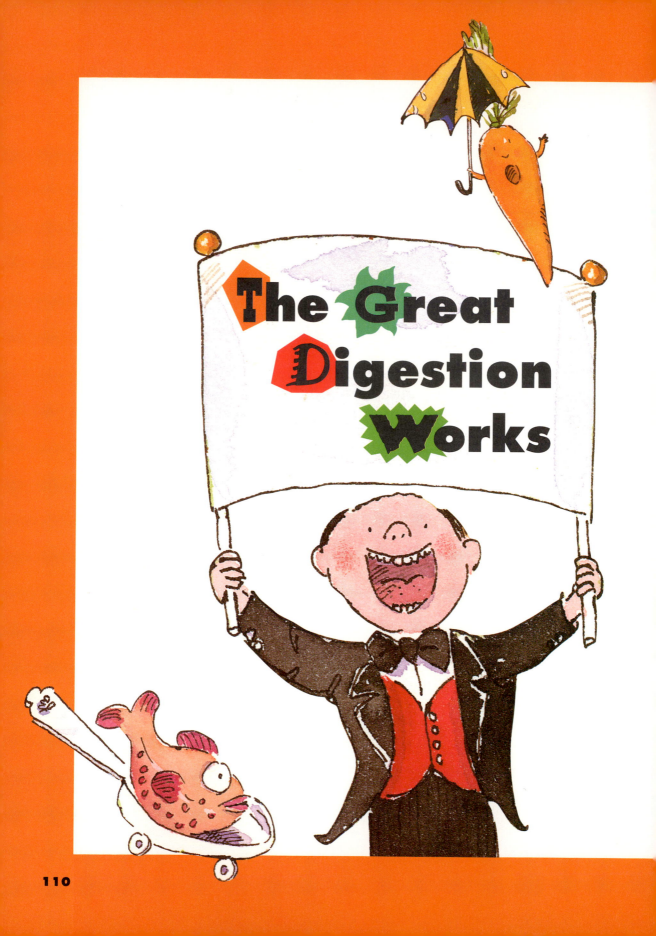

The Great Digestion Works

You can probably remember everything you ate yesterday. But do you know what happened to your food after you ate it? Well, before you gobble up your next meal and slurp down your next drink, take this ride and see what happens to your food after it's actually inside of you. With so much excitement ahead, you won't have time to snack!

The mouth, pharynx, esophagus, stomach, intestines, and rectum seem to be separate body parts, but they are all sections of one long tube, the *alimentary canal*.

Gateway to Digestion

Y ou, there! Fresh young carrot sticks! Steamy fish stew! Hop on a fork or sit in a spoon— then pass through these teeth for the ride of your life down the great *Alimentary Canal!* Are you food enough to dare?

Let the lips draw you in—see how they sip without a drip! Now, find your seats on the tongue for a quick taste test. There are more than 10,000 taste buds on the bumpy surface of the tongue, each looking for its favorite group. Be sure you find the buds waiting for you.

Inside the entrance to the canal, big things are happening. This tongue is all muscle—very flexible

Are You Food Enough to Dare to Ride the Great Alimentary Canal?

muscle. It pushes the food around and up against the bony *hard palate* (PAL iht), roof of the mouth, to prepare for more chewing and swallowing. The cheeks and lips are helping to move the food.

Meanwhile, two matching rows of teeth are chomping away. Up front, eight sharp-edged *incisors* (in SY zuhrs) are biting off mouthfuls of food. Next to them, four pointed *canines* (KAY nynz) help bite and tear the food. Behind the canines are eight premolars, or bicuspids (by KUHS pihds), and then the molars. The broad, bumpy tops of these back teeth are perfect for

Incisors

Canine

Premolars

Molars

Hard palate

Tongue

Molars

Premolars

Canine

Lip

Incisors

Entrance to the Alimentary Canal

113

grinding food. By the way, all this chewing is called *mastication* (MAS tuh KAY shuhn). Fancy name, huh?

Now, just when you thought things couldn't get wilder, three major pairs of salivary glands release their juices. They get digestion started right here in the mouth. Saliva contains amylase (AM uh layz) and mucus. *Amylase* breaks down carbohydrate foods, such as bread and pasta, into simple sugars.

Reach out and touch the inside of the cheek. It's very soft and slippery. This soft mucous membrane inside the cheeks lines the entire alimentary canal. It helps food move smoothly and prevents rough pieces from scratching.

Now, slow down! I know you're eager to see the rest of the ride, but let the teeth, tongue, and saliva do lots of good chewing and mashing. It will ease the job for the stomach down below.

BODY BULLETIN

Candy isn't the only cause of tooth decay. So are starchy snacks, such as crackers. Starchy foods that stick to your teeth can quickly turn to sugar and cause tooth decay if they aren't brushed away.

114

As a child, you have 20 "baby" teeth. By adulthood, these are replaced by up to 32 permanent teeth.

A tooth is made up of four different materials: pulp, dentin, cementum, and enamel. Deep in the sensitive heart of the tooth is the *pulp,* a soft tissue that contains the blood vessels and nerves. The pulp is made up of two parts, the pulp chamber in the center and the root canal inside the root, under your gums.

Surrounding the pulp is hard, yellow *dentin* (DEHN tihn). Most of the tooth is made of dentin, a material harder than bone. Under the gums, *cementum* (see MEHN tuhm) covers the dentin, helping to protect the root of the tooth. Covering the part of the tooth you see is the *enamel,* the shiny white surface that makes for sparkling smiles. Enamel is the hardest material in the body. It has to be hard to stand up to a lifetime of chomping and grinding.

Even with all this tough protection, teeth need help battling the destructive forces of digestion. The trouble starts when saliva leaves a wet film on the teeth. As bits of food and bacteria stick to this film, plaque is formed.

Sitting right there on the teeth, the bacteria start to work on the food, turning those bits of candy and crackers into powerful acid. The acid attacks the tooth's enamel, and soon it eats away a little hole—a *cavity.*

At first, the cavity is small and causes no pain. But act fast! A dentist can easily fill the cavity and fix the tooth at this point. Left untreated, a cavity will grow larger as decay eats down through the tooth. A toothache signals that the tooth is in real trouble—decay has reached the pulp and its nerve center deep inside. A toothache must never be ignored. An infection could set in and send bacteria out into the body, causing serious problems.

What's a tooth owner to do? To prevent serious tooth decay, follow these simple steps: Eat a healthy diet; cut down on snacks; brush at least twice a day; floss daily; and have regular checkups. When you keep your teeth clean, your saliva does the rest by rinsing the teeth all day long.

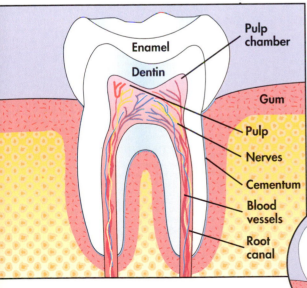

Enamel

Dentin

Pulp chamber

Gum

Pulp

Nerves

Cementum

Blood vessels

Root canal

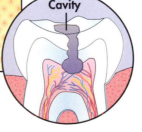

Cavity

When a healthy tooth, *above,* is overrun with bacteria, a cavity forms, *right.*

Down the Hatch

Whew! All that moving and mashing! I watched as the chunkier bites were shaped into soft balls called *bolus* (BOH lus) for swallowing. I'm only a bit of fish in the stew. I should go down easily in a slurp.

Let's see. The tongue has me up against the hard palate at the top of the mouth. The soft palate behind it is sealing off the passage to the nose before swallowing. Please, no laughing! I want to go down, not up and out the nose.

116

There's the *pharynx* (FAIR ihngks), the pathway that opens to both the stomach and the lungs. Now the epiglottis (EHP uh GLAHT ihs), a small flap of tissue, is closing off the airway to the lungs and directing me down to the *esophagus* (ee SAHF uh guhs), the long tube connecting the mouth and stomach. A gulp, and here I go!

Hey, who's pushing me? I'm being shoved along by strong muscles in the walls of the esophagus. These wavelike contractions are called *peristalsis* (PEHR uh STAL sihs). Even if this body stood on its head, I'd still be on my way to the stomach with all this power behind me.

I've only been traveling five to eight seconds, and I'm at the stomach already. I can't turn back because a ringlike muscle called a *sphincter* (SFIHNGK tuhr) closed the door that I just came through. So, forward march!

This stomach is shaped like a lazy J. Plenty of food is here already. Luckily, the stomach lining is made of lots of soft wrinkles called *rugae* (ROO jee), which

BODY BULLETIN

People often think of the stomach as the most important organ in digestion, but it isn't even necessary. Many people have had their stomach removed due to disease and have gone on to live long, healthy lives.

Muscles in the walls of the esophagus push food into the stomach.

— Bolus

— Esophagus

Stomach

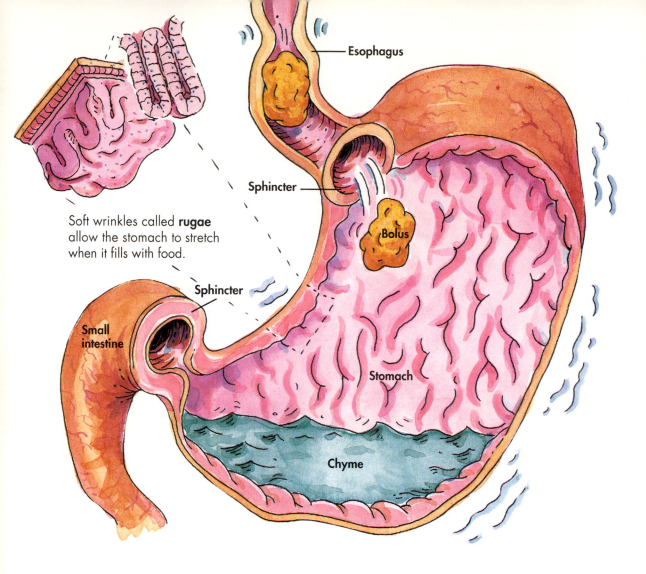

Esophagus

Sphincter

Bolus

Sphincter

Small
intestine

Soft wrinkles called **rugae**
allow the stomach to stretch
when it fills with food.

Stomach

Chyme

can smooth out to make room for more food. In fact, an adult's stomach can stretch to hold nearly 1.5 quarts (about 1.5 liters) of food.

Hey! I'm in stormy seas, being churned and pushed by the muscles in the stomach wall. Every 20 seconds I'm tossed by two kinds of waves: weak mixing waves, and strong peristaltic waves that start at the top of the stomach and squeeze everything down toward the small intestine. Still, only a few sips of thin liquid seem to be moving on at a time.

Wait, what's this? Now millions of tiny glands in the stomach walls are pouring out all kinds of powerful *gastric* (stomach) juices to break the food down into tinier and tinier pieces. These gastric juices include acids so strong that the stomach has to wear a thick mucous coating on its walls to keep from digesting itself. For protein foods, such as milk, meat, and eggs, digestion speeds up here. Starches, sugars, and fats are waiting for the next stop on our trip.

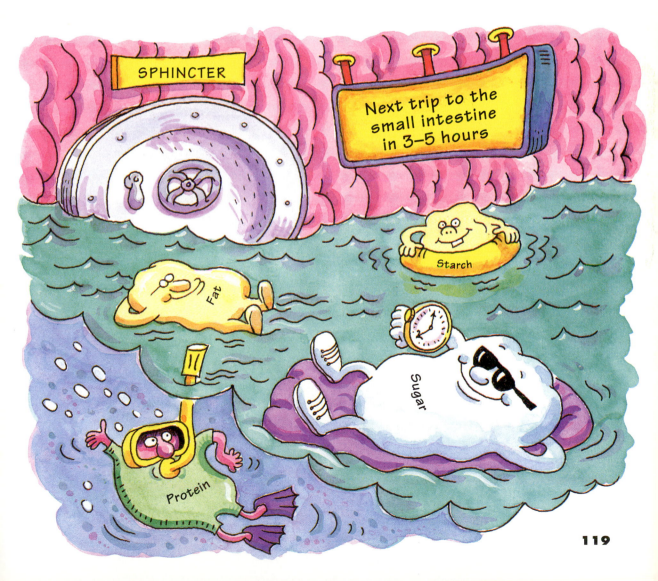

SPHINCTER

Next trip to the small intestine in 3–5 hours

Starch

Fat

Sugar

Protein

119

What's ahead? I hear that this rock-and-roll action lasts two to five hours, or until I'm chyme (kym). *Chyme* is food that is all soupy and ready to move on to the small intestine.

Well, I'm soup now. I'm ready to squirt a little at a time through the sphincter that's around the opening to the small intestine.

Somebody's cutting in line! Oh, it's just a big drink of water with some vitamins and minerals. Let them through. They don't have to be digested here at all.

SPHINCTER

Starch

Sugar

H₂O

Vitamins

Surf's up, dudes! Hang 10!

Minerals

Some**Body** you should know

WILLIAM BEAUMONT

The world got its first peek at a working digestive system quite by accident.

In 1785, William Beaumont was born in Connecticut. Early in his career, he worked as a schoolteacher, but later he became a doctor.

In 1822, as a U.S. Army surgeon, William treated Alexis St. Martin, a French-Canadian fur trader, for a gunshot wound to the stomach. The wound exposed the inside of the stomach, and the man was expected to die.

However, Alexis was hardy. He survived, but his wound never closed. Scar tissue grew around the opening but not over it. A flap of skin that covered the hole could be pushed aside to reveal the inside of the stomach. Alexis agreed to let William

Portrait of William Beaumont, in approximately 1850

observe and record the workings of his stomach as it digested various foods.

At that time, doctors did not know how the stomach broke down food. Some thought the stomach did so with intense heat; others thought it ground up food.

William found that Alexis' stomach released juice when food was present. It was this juice—which was made mostly of hydrochloric acid and pepsin (PEHP sihn)—that digested the food.

William saw that Alexis digested some foods more quickly than others. Alexis took more than five hours to digest roast pork, for example, but only one hour to digest rice.

In 1833, William published a book about the more than 200 experiments he performed on Alexis. His book is hailed as the greatest contribution ever made to our knowledge of the stomach's function. In fact, most of William's conclusions about digestion are still accepted today. His work helped launch the new science of *nutrition*, the study of how the body uses food.

The Great Food Breakdown

After all that stomach action, the small intestine may look unimportant. But some really dazzling digestion goes on there.

As soon as a bit of chyme (that's the soupy mixture that started out as food) gets to the small intestine, digestion goes into high gear. In its first few feet, the small intestine gets help from a powerful team: the pancreas (PAN kree uhs), liver, and gallbladder.

First, the pancreas pours in a mix of digestive juices that break down proteins, change starches to sugars, and split fats into smaller pieces. The small intestine helps break down these proteins, starches, and fats, by adding its own juices through thousands of tiny glands in the intestinal walls.

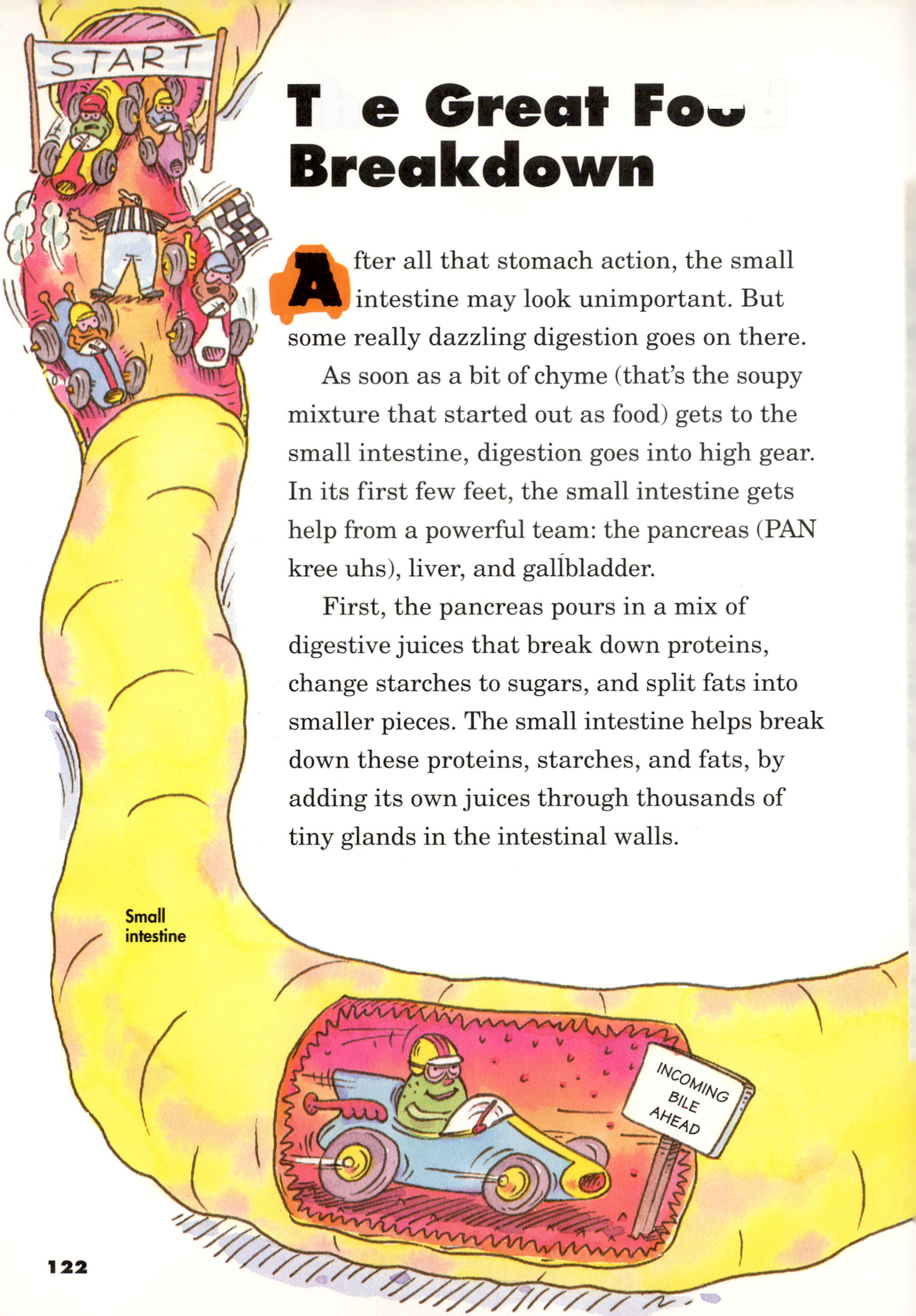

START

Small intestine

INCOMING BILE AHEAD

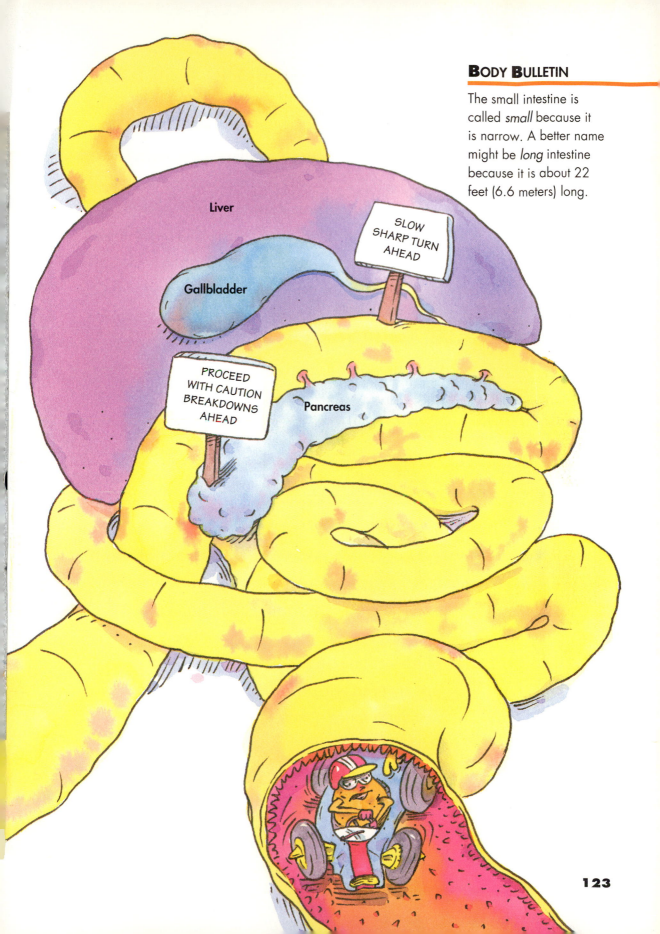

Liver

Gallbladder

Pancreas

SLOW
SHARP TURN
AHEAD

PROCEED
WITH CAUTION
BREAKDOWNS
AHEAD

BODY BULLETIN

The small intestine is called *small* because it is narrow. A better name might be *long* intestine because it is about 22 feet (6.6 meters) long.

Some gall, making me break down like that!

Must have been the bile. Heh, heh!

Next, *bile,* a liquid created by the liver and stored in the gallbladder, is released into the small intestine through the bile duct. Its strong chemicals help break down and absorb fat.

Finally, all the foods have been squeezed, churned, and dissolved into a form the body can use. Now absorption gets underway. This is a job the small intestine is perfectly designed to do.

Peristaltic waves, like those in the esophagus and stomach, keep things moving through the small intestine. A meal can travel the whole route in three to five hours, but thanks to the design of the small intestine, nothing good gets wasted.

Inside, the small intestine has ringlike folds of absorbent lining. These thousands of folds are covered with fingerlike *villi* (VIHL y), which are even more absorbent. The villi are covered with brushlike *microvilli* that aid absorption. All these parts are covered with tiny blood and *lymph* (lihmf) vessels that take the nutrients into the bloodstream. There the nutrients circulate, taking energy to every part of the body.

BODY BULLETIN

Your body takes in nutrients, such as proteins and carbohydrates. It breaks them down and uses the parts or recombines them into substances it needs. For example, proteins are used in forming skin, nails, and hair.

Meanwhile, the liver has another important job. Before heading out to the rest of the body, blood carrying the nutrients passes through the liver. The liver holds onto any extra nutrients and vitamins for later use and helps purify dangerous substances that have made it this far.

The last stop along the alimentary canal is the large intestine, or *colon* (KOH luhn). Five feet (1.5 meters) long, the large intestine is wider but much shorter than the small intestine.

The parts of food that weren't absorbed by the body are moved through the large intestine toward the rectum for disposal. As they make this final trip, water and salts that were added during digestion are absorbed back into the body.

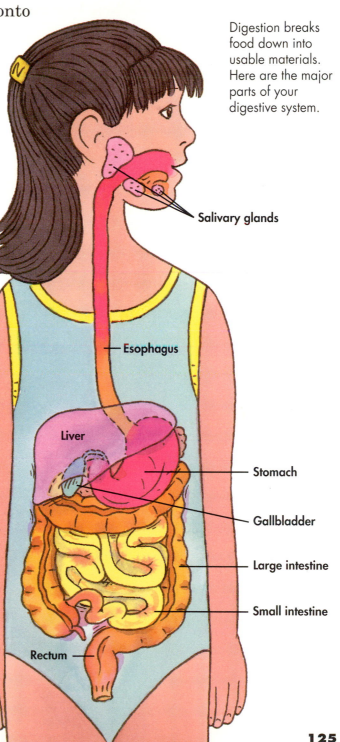

Digestion breaks food down into usable materials. Here are the major parts of your digestive system.

Salivary glands

Esophagus

Liver

Stomach

Gallbladder

Large intestine

Small intestine

Rectum

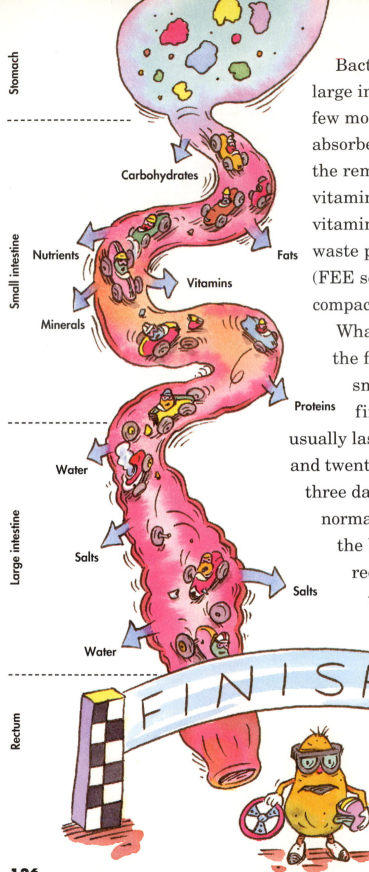

Stomach

Small intestine

Large intestine

Rectum

Carbohydrates

Nutrients

Vitamins

Fats

Minerals

Proteins

Water

Salts

Salts

Water

FINISH

Bacteria waiting in the large intestine may select a few more useful items to be absorbed. Bacteria also use the remaining food to make vitamin K and some B vitamins for the body. The waste products, called *feces* (FEE seez), become more compact as water is removed. What a slowdown after the fast run through the small intestine! This final part of the trip usually lasts between eighteen and twenty-four hours. In fact, three days is still considered normal. At last, feces leave the body through the rectum and the long trip is over.

BODYscience

Soaking It Up

Find out why the small intestine is so absorbent.

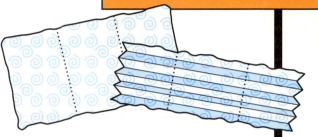

THINGS YOU NEED:

- 4 paper towels
- 2 bread pans
- a tablespoon
- a small pitcher of water
- scissors

1. Cut one paper towel to about the size of the bottom of the bread pan, or slightly larger.

2. Place the other three towels in a row. Fold them into one long accordion fold. (Fold over 1 inch [2.5 cm] along one edge, turn the sheet over and repeat until completely folded.)

3. Place the first towel over the bottom of one pan (you may have to push it down a little). Place the accordion-fold towels in the other. Use the tablespoon to add water slowly to each pan. See how much each "intestine" will absorb before water is left standing in the pan.

Like the three accordion-fold towels, the human small intestine has a great absorbing surface in a relatively small space. The many-fold absorbent layer inside the small intestine of a grown person would measure over 300 square yards (250 square meters) if stretched out flat—that's a little bigger than a tennis court!

Your Body's Waterworks

This body is my kind of place! We're talking salt water here. These humans look like they're all muscle, skin, and bones, but check inside. The number-one ingredient is salt water. Women are about 55 percent water, and men are a little soggier at about 60 percent. Babies score even higher—a newborn is about 75 percent water. If you know about water pollution, you know how tricky it is to keep such a big water system running right.

It's important for humans to keep a steady level of water, salt, and other fluids and

chemicals the body needs. Keeping this balance is more important for staying healthy than food, sleep, or anything else. If you run low on water, salt, or other fluids or chemicals—or have much too much of any—the body is in serious danger.

Ever wonder why sometimes you have lots of urine when you go to the bathroom and other times you have very little? Or why some days

55%

60%

75%

129

The urinary system, *right*, filters fluids in the body and disposes of wastes. The most important work is done by the kidneys, which filter incoming blood from arteries. Filtered blood returns to the body through veins. Wastes and water from the blood—in the form of urine—pass through the ureters to the urinary bladder. Urine leaves the body through the urethra.

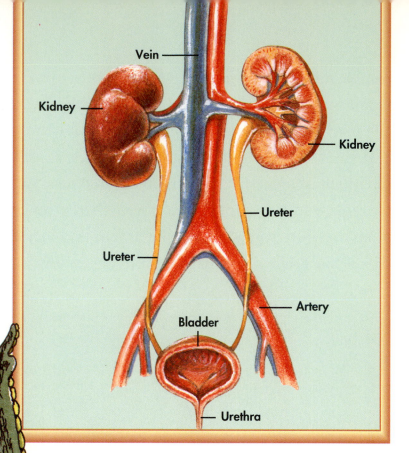

Vein

Kidney

Kidney

Ureter

Ureter

Artery

Bladder

Urethra

you drink a lot of water and don't have much urine, while on other days it's the other way around? It's because your urinary system is working to make sure you have enough—but not too much—water and salt in your body.

The *urinary system* filters fluids in the body, turns water and waste products into urine, and carries it away.

This system includes two kidneys; a bladder; two *ureters* (yoo REE tuhrz), tubes that connect the kidneys to the bladder; and a *urethra* (yoo REE thruh), the tube that runs from the bladder to the outside of the body.

The kidneys are central command in water and salt control. Every minute, day and night, about 20 percent of the blood pumped by the heart travels through the kidneys. The kidneys monitor water and salt levels, taking out exactly the right amount to keep the levels normal. They also look for important chemicals in the blood and adjust their levels as well. Special chemicals called hormones determine how much of the salt and water should be kept and how much should leave the body as urine.

The kidneys do a very complete check of the blood. Nutrients from digestion travel to all parts of the body through the bloodstream. As the body uses the nutrients to make energy,

To find your kidneys, stand up and put your hands on your hips, with thumbs touching on top of your backbone. Your kidneys are just above your thumbs, a little above your waist in the back.

Drinking enough water is as important for keeping your body healthy as are eating the right foods and getting enough sleep.

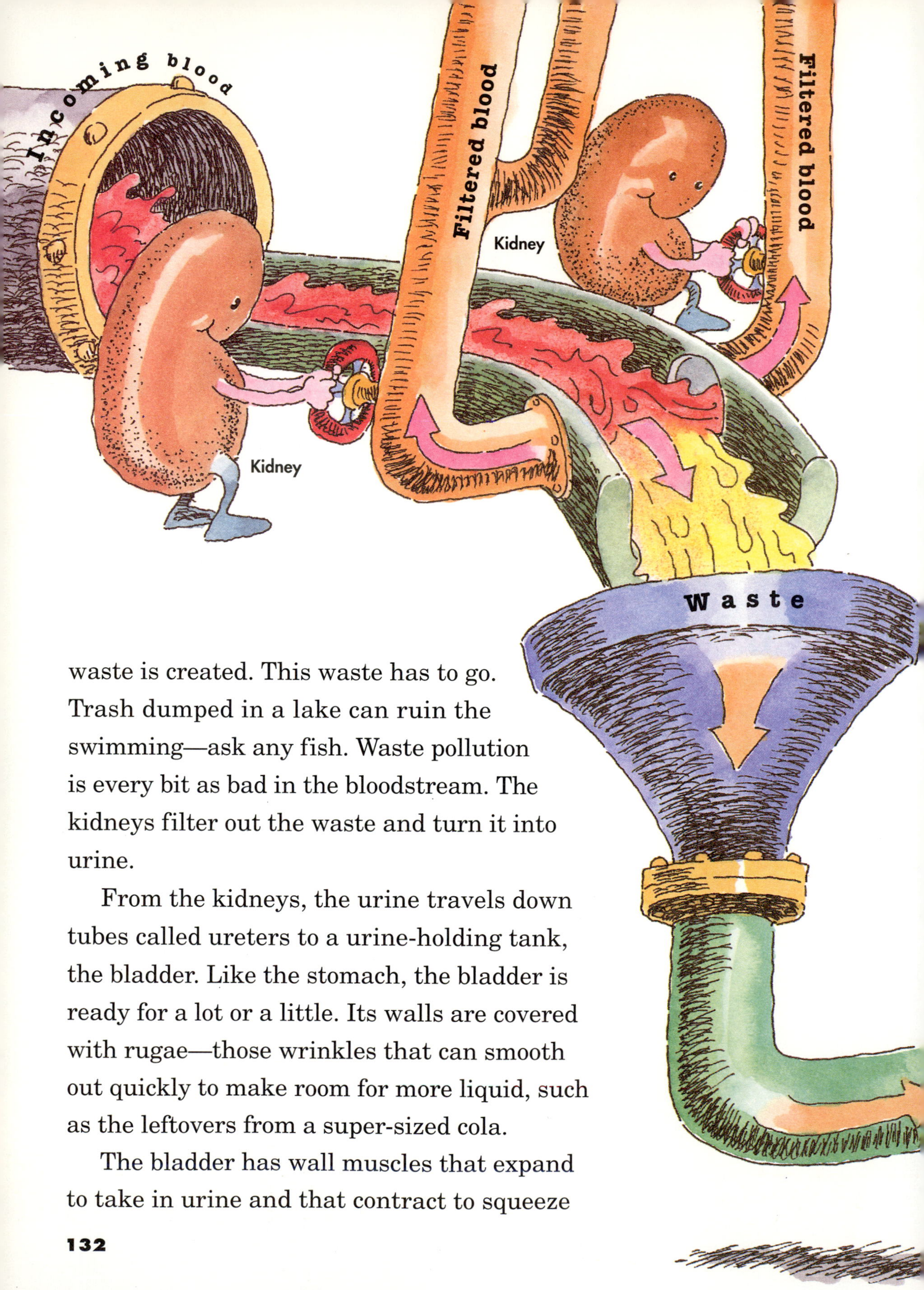

Incoming blood

Filtered blood

Filtered blood

Kidney

Kidney

Waste

waste is created. This waste has to go.
Trash dumped in a lake can ruin the
swimming—ask any fish. Waste pollution
is every bit as bad in the bloodstream. The
kidneys filter out the waste and turn it into
urine.

From the kidneys, the urine travels down
tubes called ureters to a urine-holding tank,
the bladder. Like the stomach, the bladder is
ready for a lot or a little. Its walls are covered
with rugae—those wrinkles that can smooth
out quickly to make room for more liquid, such
as the leftovers from a super-sized cola.

The bladder has wall muscles that expand
to take in urine and that contract to squeeze

it all out when it's time to urinate. When will that be? For babies, it's anytime and anywhere until they are old enough to control when they let urine go and when they make it wait.

Children and adults control when they urinate with the help of two sphincters, or rings of muscles, that shut things up tight. One is at the bladder exit. The other is just below it on the urethra, the tube that takes urine out of the body. The first one is controlled automatically. The second is the one little kids learn to control when they are toilet-trained.

Time to empty the bladder. The sphincters release, the bladder muscles squeeze, and urine flows down the urethra and out the body. Waste products are removed, and the body's water and salt levels are fine.

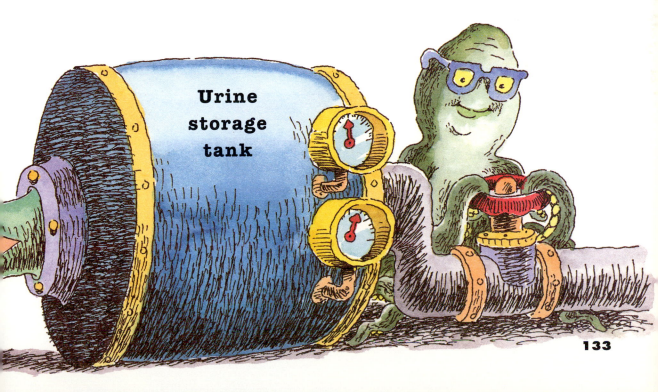

Urine storage tank

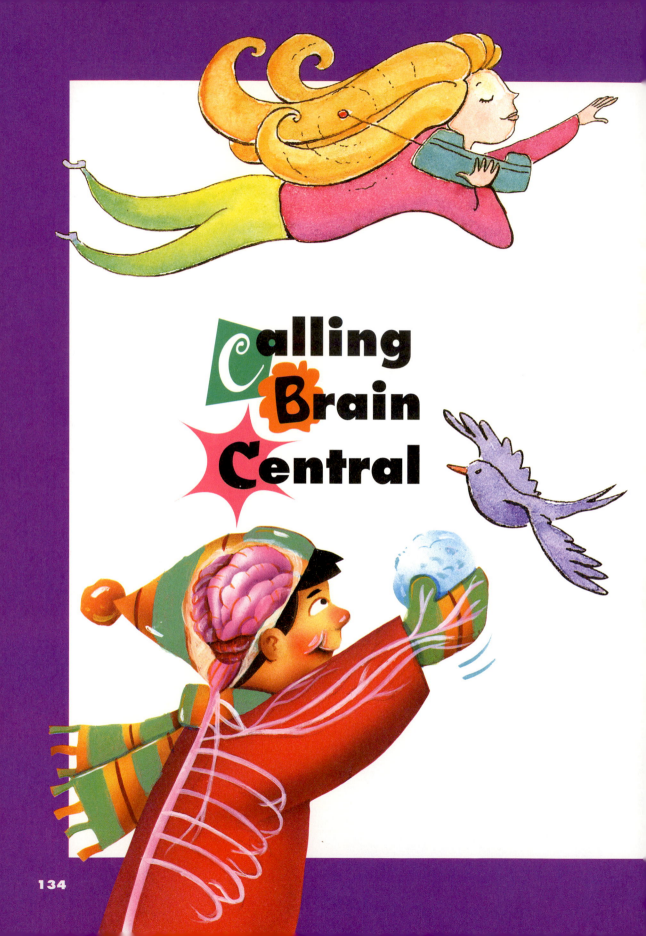

Calling Brain Central

Could you handle all the calls that come into one phone? No problem.

Could you handle all the calls that come into a million phones? Problem, big problem! But in a sense, that is just what your brain does. Every day, it receives millions of calls from your nerve cells, reacts to those calls, and sends out millions more.

Being Brainy

Ladies and gentlemen, welcome to the Puppet Playhouse! I am Marion Nett, star of almost every show. I can walk, talk, and do all kinds of tricks—as long as the puppetmaster pulls my strings! But I can't think, or move, or speak for myself because I don't have a brain, like you do.

In some ways, your brain is like a grand puppetmaster. It tells your heart to beat and your eyes to blink. It even tells you when you are hot or cold. You don't have to think about it—it just happens. But in other ways, your brain is like a wonderful tool. You can use it to move, to dream, and to plan whatever you choose.

Protected by the hard, bony case called your *skull,* your brain takes up most of the top of your head. Thin membranes and a fluid inside the skull protect and nourish the brain. When you were born, your brain weighed almost 1 pound (.45 kilogram). By the time a person is six years old, the brain is nearly its full weight, about 3 pounds (1.3 kg). And it has between 10 billion and 100 billion *neurons* (nerve cells)—no one has ever been able to count them all. Neurons send "messages"—that is, tiny electric impulses—to other nerve cells and body cells.

Compared to other animals, human beings have pretty big brains. But size isn't the most important thing when it comes to brainpower. Development is what counts, and humans have the most developed brains of all.

BODY LANGUAGE

A **CAT scan** isn't a quick look at your pet. It's a **c**omputerized **a**xial **t**omography **scan**—a special X-ray picture that shows doctors whether parts of a brain have been damaged by injury or disease.

Humans have the most developed brain of all animals.

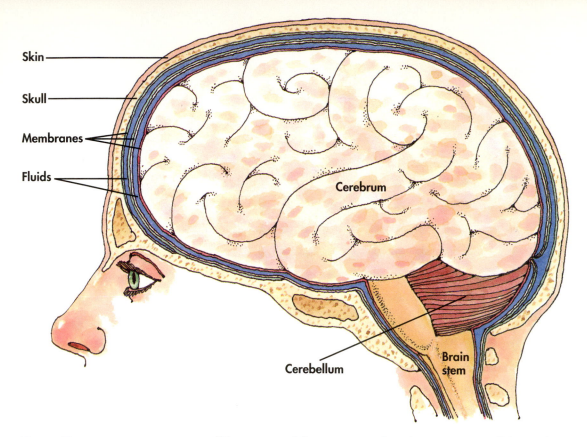

Skin

Skull

Membranes

Fluids

Cerebrum

Cerebellum

Brain stem

If you could see your brain, you would notice that it has three main parts. These are the cerebrum (SEHR uh bruhm), the cerebellum (SEHR uh BEHL uhm), and the brain stem. The *cerebrum* makes up most of your brain. Its outer layer, known as the *cortex,* is less than 1/4 inch (.6 centimeter) thick and folds into itself many times. The cortex contains the gray matter of your brain. This *gray matter* is made of neurons that let you experience emotions, get messages about the world around you—for example, from your hands, ears, and lips—and send signals to your body to react to those messages. These neurons also help you learn and think for yourself—no puppetmaster is pulling your strings. The rest of your cerebrum, beneath

your cortex, is mostly made up of nerve fibers that link the cerebrum and different parts of the brain.

Your cerebrum is divided into two *hemispheres* (HEHM uh sfirs), or halves. It's like a puppet with two sets of strings. Your left hemisphere is more involved with your math, language, and logical thinking. Your right hemisphere is more involved with your musical ability, visual thinking, and emotions. The two sides work separately, but they keep in contact through messages sent by bundles of nerve cells. If those nerve cells weren't there, your left hand wouldn't know what your right hand was doing!

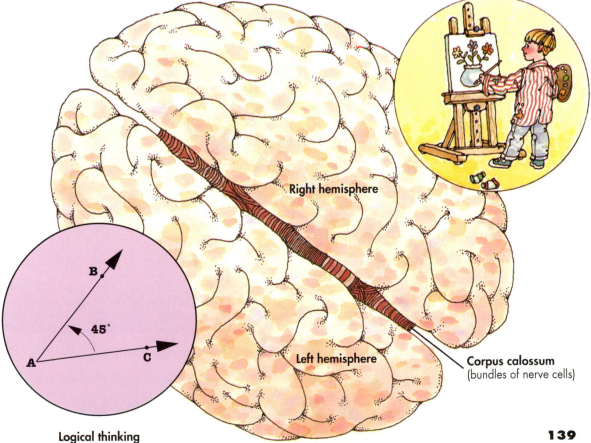

Visual thinking

Right hemisphere

Left hemisphere

Corpus calossum
(bundles of nerve cells)

Logical thinking

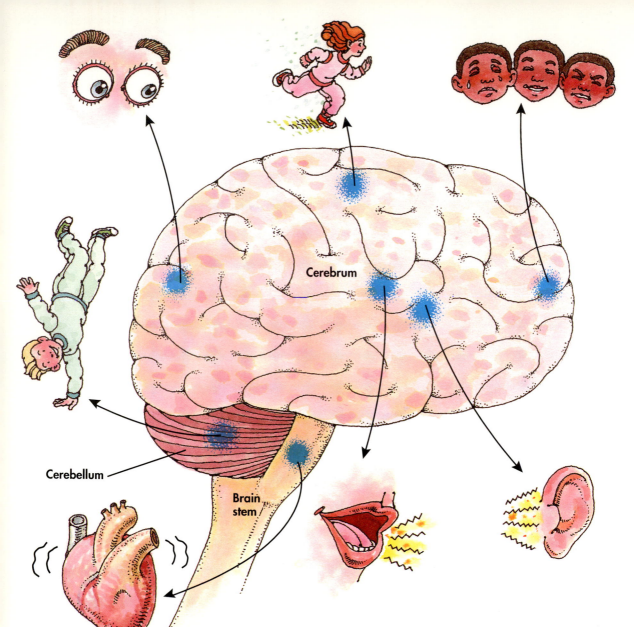

Cerebrum

Cerebellum

Brain stem

Each part of your brain has many jobs. Some are illustrated here.

Each hemisphere is divided into four *lobes,* or regions, each with many different jobs. For example, those at the back of your brain interpret signals from your eyes so that you can see. Those to the sides of your forehead help you speak, hear, and remember. Your middle lobes help your muscles move, and your frontal lobes play a major role in producing your thoughts, emotions, and personality.

Below your cerebrum is your *cerebellum,* which lets you coordinate your actions and gives you balance. It works along with your cerebrum when you play. Together, they allow you to plan actions and then carry them out.

Your *brain stem* connects your cerebrum to your spinal cord. The top part of the brain stem routes messages from your body's nerve cells to the proper part of your brain. It also sends you messages of pleasure, pain, and hunger. The middle portion of your brain stem links parts of your brain and helps your eyes make constant adjustments. The bottom of your brain stem, or *medulla oblongata,* controls important activities such as breathing and keeping your heart beating. If you had to think about such activities, you'd never have time to think about anything else.

I can't walk, talk, or dance without someone pulling my strings because I don't have a brain. So if you ever see Pinocchio, ask him to send his fairy godmother my way!

Your Nerve Networks

In many ways, your brain works like a jet pilot. It needs information—just as a pilot needs information from air traffic controllers.

Luckily, there are plenty of neurons throughout your body that are willing to do the job. In fact, your neurons send about 100 million messages a second. Like air traffic controllers, neurons use electrical impulses to send information to each other and to the brain. Your brain receives most of its messages from the spinal cord, which also transmits messages from the brain to different body parts.

All neurons are equipped with a cell body, an axon, and several dendrites. The *cell body* keeps the nerve cell alive. It is the center from which the axon and dendrites emerge.

Brain

Spinal cord

Part of major nerve network

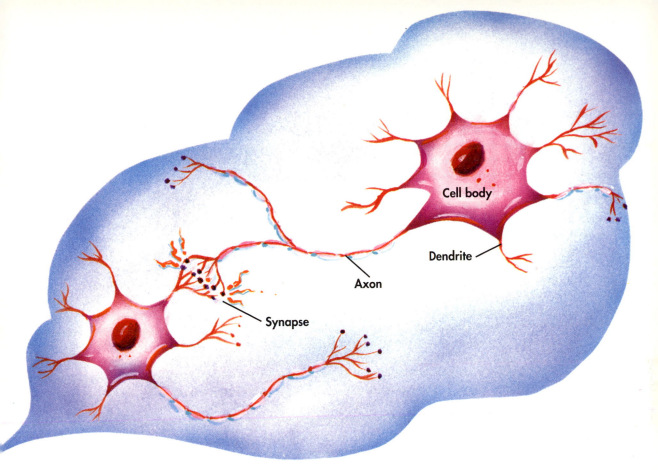

The *axon* is a fine thread that extends out of the cell body. Some axons are short. Others are up to 3 feet (91 centimeters) long. All axons end in little branches that reach out toward other cells. The ends of the branches act as transmitters by sending electrical impulses, the messages.

Dendrites are short, threadlike branches that act as the cell's receivers. They can't simply take messages from axons, however, because the two don't quite reach one another. There are tiny spaces called *synapses* between nerve cells. Dendrites catch messages that flow from other cells' axons into the synapses.

BODY LANGUAGE

Nerves are actually bundles of neuron fibers. Your **nervous system** includes networks of nerves throughout your body.

143

When you touch something hot, your hand pulls away before you have time to think. A nerve in your finger sends a pain message to your spinal cord, which causes a nerve to activate the muscles of your arm. This simple reflex doesn't involve your brain, so it happens very fast.

It seems complicated, but your nerve cells are fast. Their impulses travel up to 200 miles (322 kilometers) per hour—much slower than signals on a telephone wire, but fast enough to get from your brain to your big toe and back in a fraction of a second.

To make things even more efficient, your nerves work in teams. One team or network of nerves works automatically—as a sort of automatic pilot for the brain. Their job includes transmitting messages that tell the heart to beat at a certain rate and making sure enough blood flows to your stomach to help it digest your food.

Another network of nerves converts your plans into action. Like air traffic controllers who tell the pilot how to land safely, these nerves tell your body how to do what your brain wants— for example, how to bend down, pick up a ball, and then how to throw it.

Like a pilot, your brain takes in all the information it can get. Then it makes split-second decisions about which messages are most important. The brain is in charge of the body, but without its nervous system, it would be flying blind. With the help of the nerves, your brain can guide you through adventures day and night.

Which hand do you use for writing? If it's your right, chances are you also use that hand to throw a baseball. You also probably kick a soccer ball better with your right foot than your left. In fact, you probably do most things better with your right hand or foot than with your left. Left-handed people do everything "rightys" do, but they use their left hands and feet.

Why are some people right-handed and others left-handed? No one knows exactly, but it has a lot to do with the way your brain is divided into halves. To see how, place one finger at the top of your nose. Now trace an imaginary line over the top of your head and down the back, stopping just above your neck. You've just traced the cleft that separates the left and right hemispheres of your brain.

The nerves that carry impulses from each hemisphere cross over to the opposite side of the body. So the right hemisphere controls the left arm, the left leg, and the left side of the face. And the left hemisphere controls the right side.

Researchers believe that in right-handed people, the left hemisphere may be more developed than the right in some ways. And in left-handed people, the right hemisphere may be more developed. However, some tasks, such as typing or playing a musical instrument, require a person to use both of their hands.

A few people do just as well whether they use their right or their left hand. These people are called *ambidextrous*, a word that literally means "both skilled."

Most people do activities better with either their left hand or their right hand, *above*. However, some activities require a person to use both hands, *above right*.

Your Brain Works the Night Shift

You may think your brain goes to sleep when you do. But it doesn't. It monitors your body's functions, just as it does when you're awake. It also does things that only happen when you're asleep.

There are actually four different stages of sleep. The first stage is almost like being awake. In the second stage, your body becomes more relaxed. In the third stage, your heartbeat and your breathing slow down. Your temperature drops slightly. Your body is resting, recovering from the activities of the day. Meanwhile, your brain slows down, too. By the time you

147

reach the fourth stage of sleep, your brain is much less active than when it is awake. But you don't stay in this deep sleep very long. Your brain becomes more active, and you drift back into stage 3, then stage 2, and then stage 1. You go through this cycle several times during the night, until you awake.

Perhaps stage 1 is the most interesting time, because this is when you dream. You see pictures in your mind. Even though your eyes are closed, they move back and forth rapidly. This stage of sleep is called REM, *r*apid *e*ye

BODY LANGUAGE

Doctors use high-tech tools to find out what happens inside a person's brain. For example, an **EEG** (electroencephalogram) records a brain's electrical activity, its brain waves.

148

*m*ovement. Some scientists believe your eyes
are following the pictures you see in your brain.

During dreams, you may see people and
places you know and imagine you are having
conversations. You may even dream that you
can fly or that your dog talks to you.

No one is sure why people dream, but some
researchers believe that your dreams are based
on your wishes, fears, or desires. Sometimes
you may remember a dream when you wake
up. But you dream every night, even though
you don't always remember your dreams.

The Night Chant

Sometimes people have dreams they feel are special. This Navajo legend tells of a dream that gave a boy the power to help his people.

Long ago there were three brothers. One was a wanderer. He told wonderful tales about his journeys, but people seldom believed them. People called him Dreamer.

One day, the oldest and the youngest brothers went hunting, but they didn't take Dreamer. They took their brother-in-law instead. When they had been gone four days, Dreamer decided to follow them. He walked all day. As night was falling, he came to a canyon. Dreamer watched some crows flying around. When it was dark, he heard voices.

"Two of us were killed," said one.

"Who? Who?" said the other.

"Two disguised as a crow and a magpie were killed by hunters of the Earth people."

Dreamer realized he was hearing the gods. All night he listened while they chanted and danced. In the morning, they left. Dreamer rose and again searched for his brothers. After a short time, he found his brothers and brother-in-law. His brothers walked off. But the brother-in-law stayed and listened to Dreamer. When Dreamer told about the two creatures that had been killed, his brother-in-law said, "We *did* kill a crow and a magpie yesterday!"

Dreamer and his brother-in-law soon caught up with Dreamer's brothers. At the canyon, they saw four sheep. They drew their bows and hid.

Dreamer was closest to the sheep. Suddenly, in place of the sheep, he saw four gods. "We have come from a chant, and we are going to another. Come along," said their leader. The leader breathed on him, and he was clothed like the gods. Dreamer and the gods took four steps, turned into sheep, and bounded away.

Day and night they traveled. On the fourth day, they came to a house. Holy people and gods were coming from all directions. At midnight, the chant began. Day and night, Dreamer watched, listened, and learned. When the chant was over, he knew how to perform the ceremony. The gods let him go back to his people to teach them the ceremony and to perform it for those who were ill or had evil in their hearts. His people still hold the ceremony. They call it the Night Chant.

Some**BODY** you should know

SIGMUND FREUD

Sigmund Freud and his grandson Stefan in 1922

Of all the people who have tried to understand why people have dreams, none is more important than Sigmund Freud. Born in Austria, Sigmund was the oldest of eight children.

Sigmund began working as a medical researcher in the late 1870's. Eventually, he became a *neurologist* (noo RAH uh jihst), a doctor who treats the brain and nervous system.

Sigmund was amazed to learn how little anyone knew about mental illness. In those days, people with mental illness might be treated with mild shocks of electricity or simply told to rest or take a vacation. But Sigmund became convinced that the human brain held the key to solving mental problems.

Sigmund began looking carefully at the way people spoke and acted. He also began studying folk tales, myths, religions, and dreams. In his medical practice, he devised a therapy some people called "the talking cure."

He asked his patients to talk about anything that came to mind—their ideas, feelings, and dreams. After many sessions, some began remembering bad or troubling things. Once those memories were no longer bottled up, these patients got well.

Sigmund became convinced that people's brains store all their thoughts, feelings, and memories, whether they want them to or not. He said that dreams reveal important information about these things. For example, he said that a dream about flying might mean a person feels trapped.

At first, many people made fun of Sigmund's ideas. But over time, his work led to a new understanding of the mind. He became known as one of the founders of modern *psychiatry* (sy KY uh tree), which involves the treatment of mental illnesses.

Sense Alert

"**C**alling all muscles! Calling all muscles! Cold rain coming down—prepare to shiver. This body is getting cold!"

Messages from the world outside your skin don't come to you in exactly that way, but your brain does get constant bulletins about what's going on outside your body. All of your senses— seeing, hearing, tasting, smelling, touching, and more—get messages that travel to your brain.

Different parts of your body have nerve endings that receive different kinds of sensory (SEHN suhr ee) messages. These nerve endings are called *receptors* (rih SEHP tuhrz). For example, heat receptors in your skin tell you the rain is cold, and other receptors in your ears tell you the rain is pounding on the sidewalk.

BODY BULLETIN

Some touch receptors are grouped where you need them most. For example, you have lots of heat and cold receptors around your lips and mouth, and lots of pressure receptors in your fingertips and mouth, and near your eyes.

154

The Touch Network

If your soup is too hot or if an ant walks across your skin, you'll know about it because your touch receptors will tell you. Touch receptors are stationed over every inch of your body. Your skin contains miles of nerves and millions of touch receptors. Every touch receptor is a specialist in a certain kind of work. Some pick up on pressure —even the very light touch of a butterfly's wing. And some are triggered by pain. They're the ones that tell you to pull back from a sharp pin.

Actually, not all touch receptors are in your skin. Some in your muscles tell you if you're being pushed, pressed, or pinched. And others in your inner ears tell you whether you're tilted or straight, right side up or upside down.

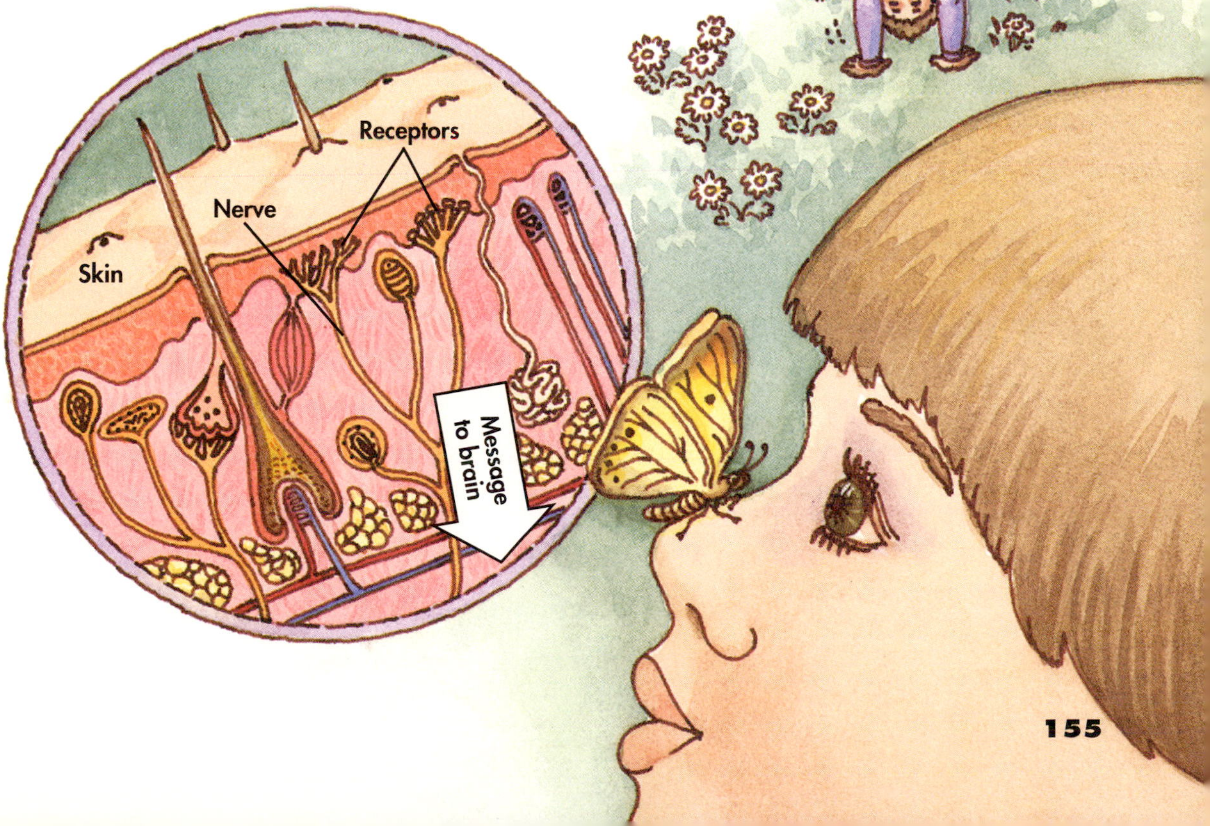

Receptors

Nerve

Skin

Message to brain

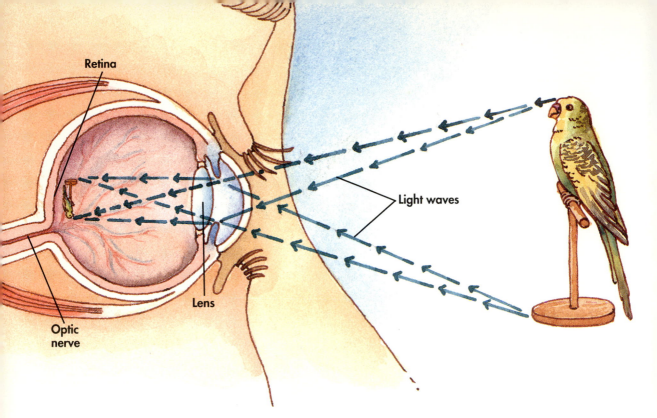

Retina

Light waves

Lens

Optic
nerve

Seeing Eye to Eye

Each of your eyes has a lens, somewhat like the lens of a camera. When you look at something, light coming into your eye passes through the lens. Your lens bends the light and focuses it on a screen of light receptors, called the *retina* (REHT uh nuh), at the back of your eyeball. But the picture on the retina is upside down. The retina turns the picture into signals that travel along the optic (AHP tihk) nerve from your eye to your brain. Part of your brain then changes the signals back into a right-side-up picture and tells you what you are seeing.

Your eyes are a few inches apart, so each gets a slightly different picture of what you see. Your brain combines the two pictures into one.

BODY BULLETIN

Your retinas have two kinds of receptor cells—rods and cones. *Rods* are sensitive to light, but not to color. *Cones* respond to different colors, but they don't work in dim light. So at night, when only your rods are working, you see objects in white, black, or gray.

Now Hear This!

When something makes a sound, it makes the air vibrate. The vibrations travel through the air in sound waves. It's the job of your ears to catch those waves.

Actually, only the outer parts of an ear catch the sound waves. Inside the ear, the sound waves make your eardrum vibrate. The eardrum passes the vibrations to three small bones that pass them to the inner ear. Your inner ear is filled with liquid and lined with cells that have tiny hairs. When the eardrum moves and the bones move, the liquid and hairs move. Then, nerve endings around the hair cells send messages to your brain and you hear the sound. Your ear closest to the sound hears it a little louder and a little sooner. When your brain compares the messages from each ear, you know where the sound came from.

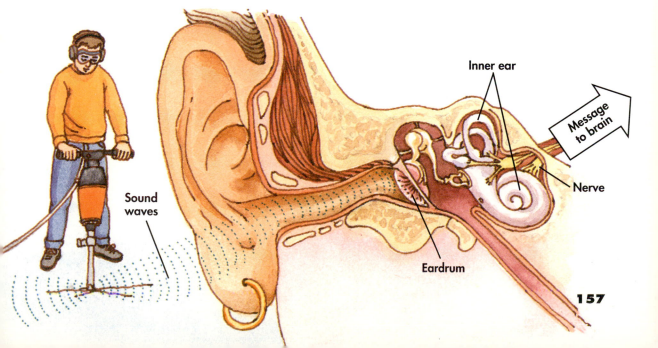

Inner ear

Message to brain

Nerve

Sound waves

Eardrum

157

What the Nose Knows

What's on the grill—hamburgers, fish, or chicken? You don't have to look to find out.

With every breath you take, your nose takes in information as well as air. You sniff in tiny particles of the chemicals that give things their smell. As the air passes through your nostrils into the hollow space at the top of your nose, it hits a membrane about the size of a dime. This membrane is filled with special receptor cells.

When particles hit the cells, they send messages to a bundle of nerve fibers. The nerves send the messages to a special part of your brain. Your brain sorts out the messages and recognizes the smell: "Yum—barbecued chicken." Or, "Uh-oh, the chicken is burning!"

Nerve

Message to brain

Particles of chemicals

Receptors

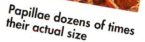

Papillae dozens of times their actual size

A Matter of Taste

Your tongue helps you talk. But it also helps you sort out tastes when you're eating.

Papillae (puh PIHL ee), the bumps on the surface of your tongue, contain groups of taste buds. Inside each taste bud are receptors that recognize different kinds of chemicals in food. When you eat, your food touches the receptors—and they send out messages. Nerves inside the tongue relay the messages to your brain.

Most of the receptor cells can recognize two or three different kinds of tastes: sweet, sour, salty, or bitter. But some groups of cells seem to specialize in certain tastes. Which tastes do you prefer?

BODY BULLETIN

Taste buds "specialize" in different tastes. That's why many people taste sweets best on the front and center, salty foods at the front left and right sides, sour foods farther back along the sides, and bitter foods at the back of your tongue.

159

BODY science

Catch the Tiger

Your eyes are a team. How do they work together? Here is a way to find out.

1. Hold this book at arm's length in front of you.

2. Look at the tiger and the cage with both eyes.

3. While you keep looking, slowly bring the book in toward your nose. What happens to the tiger?

4. Try this activity again with your own pictures. On an index card, draw or paste a picture on the left half and another picture on the right half. Look at the pictures as you bring them toward your nose. What happens?

Your brain blends what each of your eyes sees into a single picture. At most distances, your view from each eye is almost the same, so your eyes work very well together. But when you move something very close to your eyes, each eye gets quite a different view. That's why the tiger appears to be in the cage when you move this book close to your nose.

All Ears

How do your ears work together? Take turns doing this with your friends and find out.

1. Use a clock or watch with a loud tick that you can hear several feet away.

2. While you are out of the room, your friends should decide who will hold the clock or watch. Then they should stand about 6 feet (1.8 meters) apart, with their hands behind their backs and facing the door.

3. Come back into the room and walk toward your friends until you hear the ticking. Then stop and point to the friend who has the clock or watch.

4. Do the same thing again. This time, cover one ear. Is it as easy to tell who has the clock or watch? Do you have to get closer before you can guess?

Using both ears can help you locate the clock or watch more easily than using only one ear. With two messages, one from each ear, the brain gets signals it can compare. The ear that gets the signal stronger and sooner is the ear closest to the sound.

What do you think will happen if one person hides the clock or watch in the room? Will you find it faster with one or two ears? Try it.

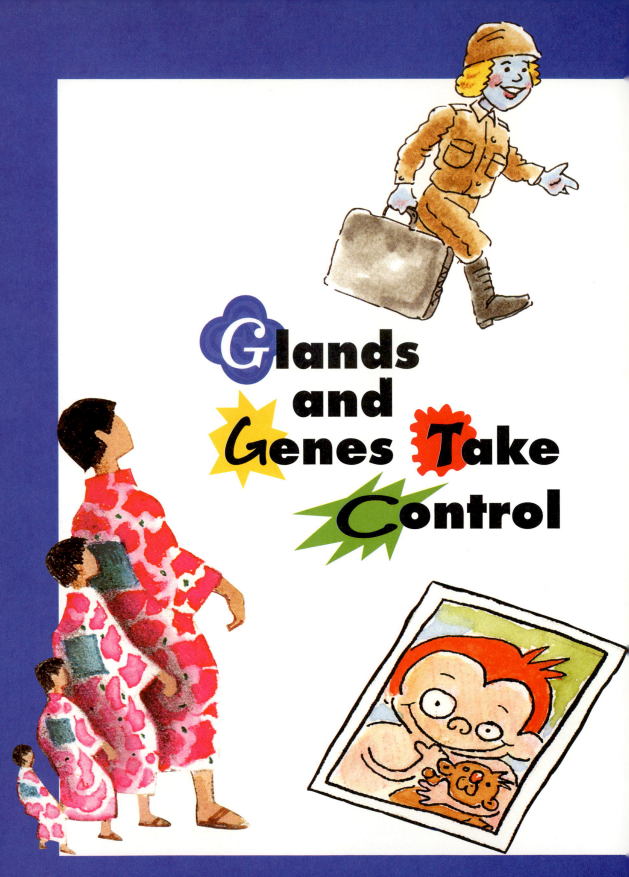

Glands and Genes Take Control

Hup one! Hup two! Your brain is in control, but it receives orders, or instructions, from other body parts. In fact, it gets many orders from your genes, and your glands help carry out those orders. Hup one! Hup two! Hup three! Hup four! Keep reading to find out more!

Your Gland Command

General Pituitary (pih TOO uh TEHR ee) in charge here! Maybe you've never heard of me, but I'm pretty big in your body. Oh, not in size—I'm only about as big as a pea—but in what I do. For a start, I make sure your body grows. I also make sure it stops growing. You'd bump your head a lot if you kept growing forever!

GENERAL PITUITARY HEADQUARTERS

YOU ARE HERE

I can make you start and stop growing because I'm a *gland*. As one of your many glands, I make some special chemicals your body uses. You have two kinds of glands. *Exocrine* (EHK suh krihn) glands make liquids such as sweat, tears, and saliva. I'm one of the other kind—an *endocrine* (EHN duh krihn) gland. Endocrine glands make chemicals called *hormones* and release them into your bloodstream. Once we pour them into your blood, things happen! For example, when I squirt growth hormone into your blood, the blood carries it to the body part that needs to grow.

BODY LANGUAGE

The word **hormone** comes from a Greek word that means "to set in motion."

And that's not all I do. I boss around some other endocrine glands. When you need their hormones, I send messages to them. I tell the glands to make hormones and to send them into the bloodstream. When you have enough of the hormones, I tell the glands to stop.

I'm the one who tells the *thyroid* (THY royd) gland in your neck to get to work. The thyroid's hormones affect how quickly your body's cells change food into heat and energy.

I'm also in charge of the sex glands, called *ovaries* in girls and *testes* in boys. These glands make girls grow into women and boys into men.

Sometimes I control the two *adrenal* (uh DREE nuhl) glands. These little glands lie just above your kidneys. Each adrenal is really two glands in one. The part I'm in charge of controls the amount of salt and glucose in your blood. *Glucose* is a sugar—your body's basic fuel. But adrenal glands do other things without my say-so. Did a friend ever jump out at you when you didn't expect it? Your heart started pounding, your breathing got faster, and blood rushed to your head. These things happened because your adrenal glands got a signal that you were in danger. The glands produce a hormone known as *adrenaline* (uh DREHN uh lin) to help prepare your body to fight or run.

Some Important Endocrine Gland Headquarters

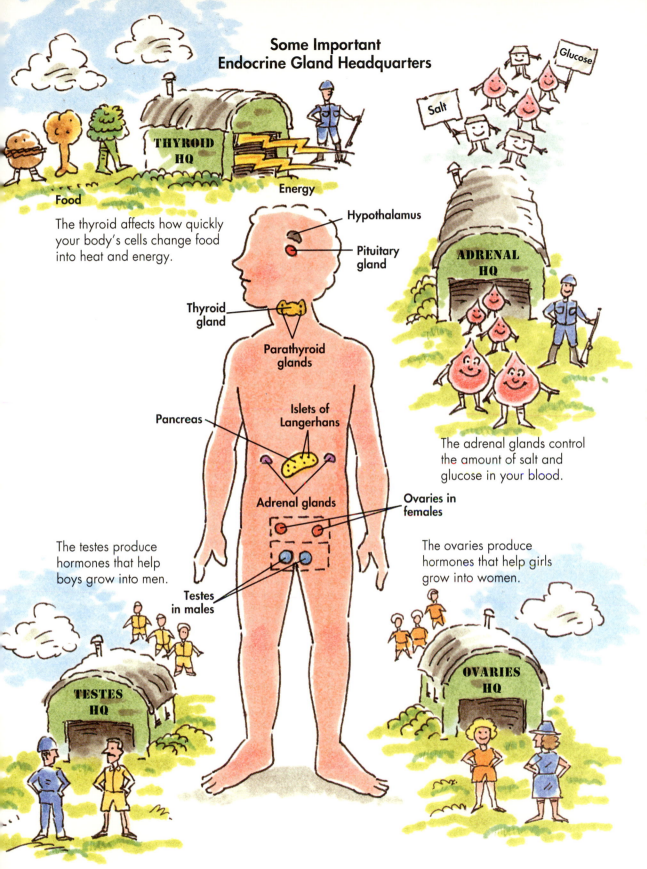

THYROID HQ

Food

Energy

The thyroid affects how quickly your body's cells change food into heat and energy.

Glucose

Salt

Hypothalamus

Pituitary gland

ADRENAL HQ

Thyroid gland

Parathyroid glands

Pancreas

Islets of Langerhans

The adrenal glands control the amount of salt and glucose in your blood.

Adrenal glands

Ovaries in females

The testes produce hormones that help boys grow into men.

Testes in males

The ovaries produce hormones that help girls grow into women.

TESTES HQ

OVARIES HQ

Some of the endocrine glands outside of my control are the four *parathyroids,* near the thyroid. These four glands control the amount of calcium and phosphate in your body.

Then there are the tiny *islets of Langerhans.* These special cells are scattered throughout your pancreas, which helps you digest food.

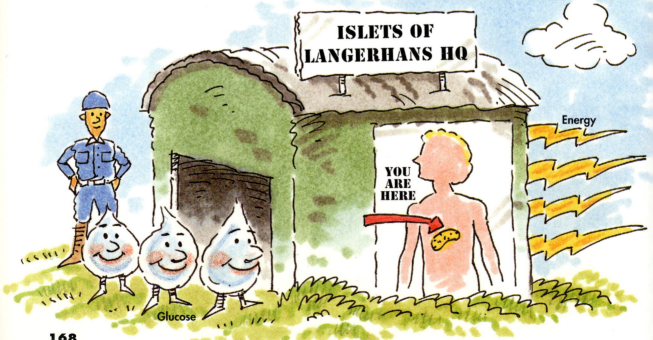

The islets of Langerhans produce the hormone *insulin* (IHN suh lihn). Because of insulin, your cells can convert glucose into energy.

I guess by now you realize I'm top gland. That's why I'm General Pituitary. But like many generals, I take orders from my commander in chief. This commander in chief is a part of your brain called the *hypothalamus* (HY puh THAL uh muhs). When your hypothalamus receives messages from the nervous system, it produces *releasing hormones*. These releasing hormones tell me to get to work. Some are heading my way now, so here I go—back into action!

The One-Inch Boy

Many cultures have folk tales about children who stay tiny. This one comes from Japan.

Once there lived a boy who was only one inch tall. But he was not short of spirit. He was *Issun-boshi,* The One-Inch Boy. One morning, he grabbed a needle for a sword and set out to see the world.

After hacking his way through long grass, Issun-boshi came to a river. He hopped into a rice bowl and, using a chopstick, paddled across.

When he reached the capital city, he found work in a palace. The princess who lived there loved the tiny boy. They played every day.

One day, as they walked to the temple, a demon roared: "I will eat you!" The demon had three eyes, three horns, three toes, and three fingers—all green. It waved a spike-covered club. Issun-boshi seized his needle-sword and ran right up the demon. He jabbed its great, green nose and moist, green tongue. The demon howled and spat Issun-boshi into a tree. Then it dropped its club and vanished.

The princess plucked Issun-boshi from the tree. She knew demons' clubs are magic. She swung the club, crying, "Let Issun-boshi grow tall!" And he did—one inch for every swing of the club. The princess and Issun-boshi's friendship also grew. Years later, they married.

You can't wave a club to grow tall, but your body's glands can help you grow.

Gregor Mendel is my name. I'm crazy about peas–pea plants, to be precise. I was born in 1822, and I was a good student. When I was a monk in Austria, back in the mid-1800's, I studied peas. Thanks to my pea plants, we can explain such things as why people have blue eyes or dark skin.

I wondered why some pea plants in the garden grew tall and others short. Why were some peas wrinkled and others smooth? Why were some yellow and others green?

I *crossed* (bred) plants with different traits, such as height or seed color. One time when I crossed a tall pea plant with a short one, all their baby plants were tall. I thought the "short" trait had disappeared. But then I crossed two of the tall baby plants. Three out of every four of their baby plants were tall, and one was short. The "short" trait hadn't disappeared! It just was hidden for a while.

From this, I learned that parents pass traits to their babies in some sort of package. Today, you call that package a *gene,* and the passing of traits is called *heredity.*

In my peas, I saw that the "tall" gene controlled the height. So I called the

Gregor Mendel

"tall" gene *dominant* and the "short" gene *recessive.*

But how did the "short" gene come back? Maybe the tall parents had two "tall" genes, and the small parents two "small" genes. Then, each baby plant got two genes for height, one from each parent. Plants with a tall parent and a short parent had a "tall" gene and a "short" gene. The "tall" gene was dominant, so they were tall. But when those plants had babies of their own, a baby sometimes got two "short" genes. So it was short.

I wrote a report on all this in 1866. Today, I get the credit for starting the study of heredity, *genetics.*

You've Got the Look

Do you ever wonder why all your sisters have red hair? Or why you have freckles but your cousin doesn't? It's all because of DNA.

DNA carries a code for your skin color and other physical traits. Unless you have an identical twin, no one else has your exact DNA.

DNA is too small to see, but it looks like a long, twisted ladder. It's located inside your *chromosomes* (KROH muh sohms), which are in the nucleus of your cells.

The rungs of the ladder in DNA make up *genes,* which store your code. Genes are inherited from your family. You got them from your parents, who got them from their parents.

Nucleus

Chromosome

Human body cell

DNA

Gene

Your physical characteristics—such as your height, your eye color, and your skin color—are determined by genes in DNA.

BODY LANGUAGE

Chromosomes are tiny, threadlike parts of a cell's nucleus. Most human cells have 46 chromosomes. Chromosomes are made mostly of DNA and proteins, and they carry genes.

173

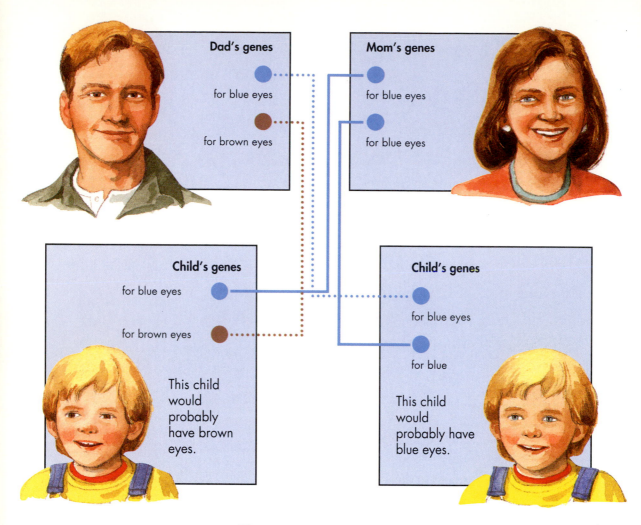

Dad's genes

for blue eyes

for brown eyes

Mom's genes

for blue eyes

for blue eyes

Child's genes

for blue eyes

for brown eyes

This child would probably have brown eyes.

Child's genes

for blue eyes

for blue

This child would probably have blue eyes.

Your genes come in pairs, one from each parent. When the two genes are different, the trait of only one gene shows up. This gene is *dominant* (DAHM uh nuhnt). The other is *recessive* (rih SEHS ihv).

If your mom gave you a gene for blue eyes and your dad gave you a gene for brown eyes, your eyes are probably brown. That's because the gene for blue eyes is recessive. You still have a gene for blue eyes—you just don't see that trait. However, if you received two genes for blue eyes, then you probably have blue eyes.

Today, your body has trillions of cells. DNA is in all of them, carrying your code. But once you had only one cell. That cell divided in two, those two divided in four, and so on. DNA gave each cell your code. Just before the first cell divided, the ladder split down the middle. Each half rebuilt. The cell then had two DNA ladders exactly alike. So when the cell divided, each cell got one DNA ladder. This happened again and again. DNA then ordered the cells to specialize—for example, to become part of your blood, liver, backbone, or toes.

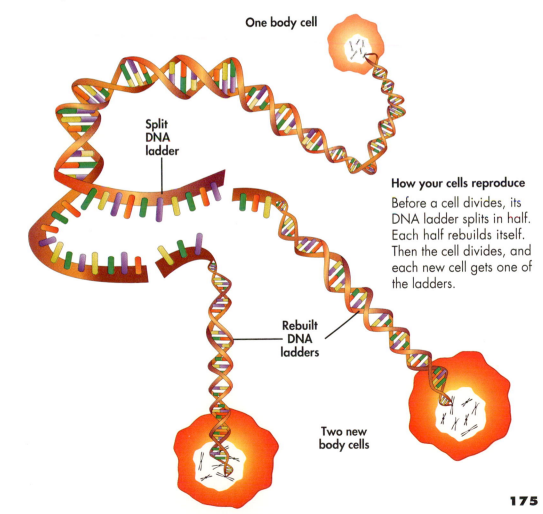

One body cell

Split DNA ladder

Rebuilt DNA ladders

Two new body cells

How your cells reproduce

Before a cell divides, its DNA ladder splits in half. Each half rebuilds itself. Then the cell divides, and each new cell gets one of the ladders.

DNA also tells your body to make proteins. *Proteins* are one of the main building blocks of cells. If your body needs a hormone that is a protein, DNA has the code. But proteins are made outside the nucleus. So part of the job is done by another substance called RNA. The DNA ladder unravels and splits down the middle. It builds a strand of *messenger RNA*. Messenger RNA copies the code and leaves the nucleus. Then the DNA ladder rebuilds.

The messenger RNA travels to the part of your cell that builds proteins. That part of the cell "reads" the code and "orders" the right kinds of molecules to make the protein. When the molecules arrive, they are assembled in the same order as the code on the messenger RNA. The molecules link up, building the protein you need!

Nucleus of body cell

DNA ladder

Messenger RNA

Code reader

New protein

Molecules

Some**BODY** you should know

BARBARA McCLINTOCK

Barbara McClintock was born in 1902, two years after the science of genetics began. Throughout her life, she did much to make this new science grow.

To help explain how people pass traits to their children, Barbara studied how corn plants pass traits. Corn has ten chromosomes. These carry genes that decide the corn's traits. As a college student in the 1920's, Barbara found ways to identify each corn chromosome and ways to find out which genes were on each one.

Later, she grew special corn that had waxy, purple kernels. The two traits were carried by the ninth chromosome. She crossed this corn with a kind that had a different ninth chromosome. Some of the baby corn had kernels that were purple but not waxy, and some had kernels that were waxy but not purple. In addition, she found that their ninth chromosome had a new shape! The experiment helped prove that chromosomes trade parts to mix traits in new ways. This discovery was hailed as a cornerstone of genetics.

Barbara later studied what happens when chromosomes are broken by X rays. She found that the damage done to chromosomes is sometimes controlled by other genes. She also discovered that these genes can jump to other chromosomes and turn them on and off.

At first, her idea about jumping genes was too new for most scientists. They ignored it until the 1960's, when other scientists using different techniques proved her observations to be right.

Barbara received the 1983 Nobel Prize for medicine and physiology for discovering the mobility of genes. She went on researching genetics until her death in 1992.

Barbara McClintock researching corn traits in the early 1950's

BODYscience

A Genetic History

Try tracing your family's genetic history.

1. To start a genetic history, think about your relatives. Do some have the same traits, such as dark, curly hair? Tiny hands? Certain allergies? Jot down a few traits and the names of relatives who have them.

2. Interview the people on your list. Ask who else in the family has had the same traits. Use an audiotape, videotape, or paper and pen to record the answers.

3. Go as far back in your family history as you can. Look in photo albums for other relatives who had the traits, and read old letters or clippings for clues.

4. Tell the genetic story! Draw a family tree showing how the traits were passed down.

OUR FAMILY

Your Own History

Record your own history.

1. Look for things that tell something about you–a baby book, baby clothes, old photos, or drawings or "writing" you did when you were little.

2. Make a list of people who can tell you what you were like and what you did when you were younger. Interview the people on your list. Audiotape, videotape, or write down their answers.

3. Jot down some notes of your own about yourself. For example, what have you done in school? What have been your favorite toys?

4. How have you changed? Has your hair changed? Your favorite toys? Your home? Your friends? Write a story, make a book, or tell a story on audiotape or videotape based on your own history. Share the story with relatives or friends.

Running a Healthy You

It doesn't matter if they are spiders in the attic, trees in the rain forest, or the king and queen of the United Kingdom—all living things have requirements to stay healthy. What are yours? You need sleep, water, air, nutrients, and exercise to run a healthy you.

Nutrients Your Body Needs

After 3,000 years as a mummy, I know a thing or two about preserving bodies. Here's the secret of a long life: Eat right. It's important to eat right because your body needs certain amounts of proteins, carbohydrates, fats, vitamins, and minerals.

All your body parts are made of protein. Your body needs protein every day to grow and to repair itself. You can get protein from animal foods— such as meat, fish, eggs, poultry, and dairy products. You can also get protein from combinations of certain plant foods, such as whole-wheat bread and peanut butter. Without protein, your muscles sag, your hair grows dull, and you lose your pep.

In addition to proteins for body building, you need carbohydrates for fuel. Some foods supply simple carbohydrates, also called simple sugars. For example, fruit and honey supply fructose (FRUHK tohs). Milk, cheese, and yogurt supply lactose (LAK tohs). Table sugar and syrups supply sucrose (SOO krohs). The body quickly absorbs these sugars and burns

BODY BULLETIN

How much protein you need depends on your age and size. Children need between 16 and 60 grams a day. A cup of yogurt, a peanut butter sandwich, a chicken breast, and three glasses of milk supply more than a day's protein for an average eleven-year-old.

182

them for energy. Complex carbohydrates, also called starches, are found in grains, pasta, and certain vegetables, such as beets, carrots, potatoes, and dried kidney beans. Starches break down more slowly than simple sugars in the body, so they provide longer lasting energy. A third kind of carbohydrate, called fiber, is found in bran, the stems of leafy vegetables, and the skins of fruits. Fiber is too tough to digest, but it adds bulk to food and helps push it through your intestines.

Besides protein and carbohydrates, you need some fats. Your body makes fats from the sugars and starches it does not use right away. It also obtains fats from animal foods and many plant foods—nuts, olives, and avocados, for example. Fats store extra energy and make up parts of your lungs, heart, nerves, skin, and hormones. They pad some organs, such as your liver, as well as your hands, feet, and buttocks. They also help your body absorb certain vitamins.

Vitamins are special chemicals found in food. Inside your body, they spark the reactions that change proteins, carbohydrates, and fats into tissues and energy. But these are only a few of the jobs vitamins do. The chart on the following pages lists more.

BODY LANGUAGE

Bran is the coating on grains such as wheat and oats. It supplies fiber and vitamin B_6. This coating is removed when making white flour or meal, so whole-grain baked goods are your best sources of this nutrient.

VITAMIN MARKET

VITAMIN A (RETINOL)

HELPS GIVE YOU BOUNCY HAIR, GLOWING SKIN, AND BETTER NIGHT VISION.

SOME SOURCES: MILK, LIVER, FISH-LIVER OIL, GREEN LEAFY VEGETABLES, ORANGE AND YELLOW FRUITS AND VEGETABLES

VITAMIN B_1 (THIAMINE)

HELPS KEEP YOUR NERVOUS SYSTEM AND DIGESTIVE TRACT RUNNING SMOOTHLY.

SOME SOURCES: WHOLE-GRAIN BREADS AND CEREALS, NUTS, DRIED BEANS, PORK

VITAMIN B_2 (RIBOFLAVIN)

HELPS YOUR BODY USE PROTEINS, FATS, AND CARBOHYDRATES; MAINTAINS MUCOUS MEMBRANES IN YOUR BODY.

SOME SOURCES: MILK, LIVER, FISH, AVOCADOS, LEAFY GREEN VEGETABLES

VITAMIN B_3 (NIACIN)

HELPS YOUR BODY CELLS USE NUTRIENTS; LOWERS CHOLESTEROL IN THE BLOOD.

SOME SOURCES: WHOLE GRAINS, DRIED PEAS AND BEANS, EGGS, NUTS, FISH, LIVER, POULTRY, KIDNEY

VITAMIN B_6 (PYRIDOXINE)

HELPS YOUR BRAIN WORK; HELPS YOUR BODY PRODUCE ENERGY FROM PROTEIN.

SOME SOURCES: MOLASSES, WHOLE GRAINS, WHEAT GERM, FISH, NUTS, LIVER, BANANAS, POTATOES

VITAMIN B_{12} (COBALAMIN)

HELPS THE GROWTH OF RED BLOOD CELLS; KEEPS NERVE CELLS HEALTHY.

SOME SOURCES: MILK, EGGS, CHEESE, FISH, MOST MEATS

BIOTIN

HELPS YOUR BODY USE CARBOHYDRATES, FATS, AND PROTEINS.

SOME SOURCES: MILK, EGG YOLKS, KIDNEY, LIVER, NUTS, PEAS

PANTOTHENIC ACID

HELPS YOUR BODY USE CARBOHYDRATES, FATS, AND PROTEINS; HELPS YOUR BODY RESPOND BETTER TO STRESS.

SOME SOURCES: ALMOST ALL FOODS, INCLUDING LIVER, KIDNEY, RAW GREEN VEGETABLES, AND WHOLE-GRAIN BREADS AND CEREALS

FOLIC ACID

HELPS YOUR RED BLOOD CELLS GROW; HELPS KEEP YOUR HAIR AND FINGERNAILS STRONG.

SOME SOURCES: LIVER, ORANGE JUICE, PEAS, DRIED BEANS, DARK-GREEN LEAFY VEGETABLES

VITAMIN C (ASCORBIC ACID)

HELPS WOUNDS HEAL; HELPS TO FORM *COLLAGEN*, A PROTEIN FOUND IN SKIN, BONES, AND OTHER TISSUES.

SOME SOURCES: CITRUS FRUITS, GUAVAS, STRAWBERRIES, CANTALOUPE, POTATOES, RAW CABBAGE, TOMATOES, GREEN PEPPERS

VITAMIN D

HELPS KEEP YOUR BONES STRONG AND STRAIGHT.

SOME SOURCES: FORTIFIED MILK, FISH-LIVER OILS, ALSO SUNLIGHT

VITAMIN E (TOCOPHEROL)

HELPS FORM RED BLOOD CELLS AND OTHER TISSUES.

SOME SOURCES: VEGETABLE OILS, WHEAT GERM

VITAMIN K

HELPS YOUR BLOOD CLOT SO THAT CUTS AND SCRAPES HEAL.

SOME SOURCES: CHEESE, LIVER, SOYBEANS, GREEN LEAFY VEGETABLES

DOES A PIECE OF CARROT CAKE COUNT AS A SERVING OF VEGETABLES?

Fats, Oils,
& Sweets
USE SPARINGLY

● Fat (Naturally occurring
and added)
▼ Sugars (Added)

Milk, Yogurt, &
Cheese Group
2-3 SERVINGS

Meat, Poultry, Fish,
Dry Beans, Eggs,
& Nuts Group
2-3 SERVINGS

Vegetable Group
3-5 SERVINGS

Fruit Group
2-4 SERVINGS

Bread, Cereal, Rice, & Pasta Group   **6-11 SERVINGS**

Be sure to eat the proper foods to get the vitamins you need, but also remember to include minerals—substances such as calcium, iron, potassium, and zinc—in your meals, too.

To get potassium, drink orange juice or add bananas to your cereal daily. Potassium helps your nerves, muscles, and heart work smoothly. Include meat, seafood, eggs, nuts, peas, or beans in your meals because they contain zinc. Zinc helps your body put proteins together. Too little zinc results in a poor appetite, slow-healing sores, and never-ending colds. Include milk, cheese, yogurt, or green leafy vegetables at each meal to get enough calcium. Calcium builds strong bones and teeth. It also calms your nerves and helps you sleep.

How do you know you are taking in all the nutrients you need? The food pyramid shown on the previous page is one handy guide for eating right. Every day, count the number of servings you eat from each group on the pyramid. If you're short in one group—fruits, for example—have some before bedtime. And vary the foods you eat so that you are more likely to get all the nutrients you need. With the pyramid to guide you, maybe your body will last as long as mine.

BODY LANGUAGE

LDL (low-density lipoprotein) is scientists' name for the "bad" cholesterol that clogs your blood vessels. *HDL* (high-density lipoprotein) is their name for the "good" cholesterol that helps prevent clogging of the arteries.

The food pyramid on the previous page is one guide to eating right. It recommends having fewer portions of the foods near the top—such as sweets, cheeses, and nuts—and more of the foods near the bottom—such as fruits, rice, and pasta.

187

Sugary foods can make you tired.

Pies, cakes, candies, ice cream—what are the best-tasting foods you know? Foods like these taste good, but they often have so much sugar and fat that they are bad for you if you eat too many of them.

Your body needs sugar and fat for energy. In fact, it makes fat and glucose from carbohydrates you eat. However, too much extra sugar and fat in your diet can make you tired. And it's easy to get too much—just one can of soda has as much as 10 teaspoons of sugar. Many people take in a cup of sugar a day!

What happens when you take in too much sugar? The blood absorbs simple sugars quickly. A sharp increase of sugar in the blood signals the pancreas to pour out insulin. Insulin makes your liver and muscles take sugar from the blood to store it. So the sugar is changed to fat.

A fatty diet also can overload your body. Fats from animals contain cholesterol. Such fats include butter and egg yolks in baked goods. You need some cholesterol to produce hormones and to coat nerves, but your liver makes

Fatty foods can make you tired and can give you bad cholesterol.

enough to meet these needs. Cholesterol from animal fats, on the other hand, causes problems. Chunks of this "bad" cholesterol often stick to the walls of blood vessels, causing the vessels to narrow. As a result, the chunks slow down the flow of blood and its life-giving oxygen. This can cause tiredness, leg pains, chest pains, and heart attacks.

Too much fatty food can damage the heart in another way when it causes extra weight gain. An overweight person's heart must pump blood through miles of blood vessels in extra fat tissue. In time, the heart may give out from overwork.

Once in a while, you still may eat those "best-tasting" foods. But when you eat them, remember four magic words: "Just a little, please."

Some**BODY** you should know

CHRISTIAAN EIJKMAN

Christiaan Eijkman's chickens helped prove the importance of a proper diet for humans.

In the late 1800's, after the French chemist Louis Pasteur proved that germs cause disease, scientists rallied to fight germs. Among them was a Dutch doctor, Christiaan Eijkman (EYEK mahn).

While in the army, in what is now Indonesia, Christiaan saw people suffering from a disease called beriberi. In 1886, he joined a medical team to look for the germ that caused it. After two years, the rest of the team returned to Europe. Christiaan stayed and headed a school for doctors.

He still hoped to find the germ and show that it spread the disease from sick animals to healthy ones. But his experiments failed. Then some chickens became sick. Their illness looked like beriberi. But when Christiaan began to study them, they immediately became well.

Christiaan looked for a reason to explain this. He learned that a cook had fed the birds white rice. When the cook left his job, a new cook fed the birds brown rice—rice with its coating still on. Christiaan realized that the birds had been sick only while on the white-rice diet. He did more experiments. Over and over, he produced beriberi by feeding chickens white rice and cured it by giving them brown rice.

If germs did not cause beriberi, what did? He thought that white rice was poisonous and that something in the coating on brown rice made the poison harmless. He was wrong. Scientists later found that parts of certain foods, such as the brown coating on rice, contain substances vital to health. They named these substances the B vitamins.

Still, Christiaan was the first to show that a diet missing important parts of food causes disease. He won the 1929 Nobel Prize for medicine for discovering vitamins that prevent beriberi.

Shaping Up

Many of the things you do every day, including some sports, require only short bursts of activity. However, to keep yourself going—and enjoy being active—you need flexibility, strength, and endurance. In short, you need to shape up. Exercise does that.

Flexible muscles and tendons help you reach that extra inch. But as you get older, muscles and tendons lose their flexibility, and they tighten unless you exercise them. So get to work and loosen up those muscles. Think: To make tight shoes fit, you stretch them. Stretching works on tight muscles, too.

Before you stretch, however, warm up. Skip rope or jog in place. This increases the blood flow to your muscles and tendons and warms them. Warm muscles stretch more easily than cold ones and are less likely to get hurt.

To strengthen your muscles, use them for lifting. Lifting weights is good for athletes, but it can injure muscles that are still growing. So lift your body instead. Chin-ups and

pushups strengthen your arms. You can do sit-ups or "crunches" to strengthen your abdomen. Lifting or bending your legs strengthens your muscles, too.

Strong arms and legs may get you going, but a strong heart and strong lungs will keep you going. A strong heart and lungs can deliver oxygen to your body more efficiently for lasting energy and an alert mind. In other words, they give you endurance, staying power.

You can exercise your heart and lungs with *aerobic exercise*—that is, any activity which lasts 20 minutes or longer, increases the amount of oxygen your lungs take in, and raises your heart rate.

BODY LANGUAGE

Aerobic comes from the Greek words for "air" and "life." Exercises that require you to inhale a lot of air for a long time are aerobic. Short-term exercises don't build up your intake of oxygen. So they are called **anaerobic**, which comes from the Greek words for "no air" and "life."

191

Such activities include walking fast, running, swimming, cycling, and jumping rope. Choose aerobic activities that you enjoy. Do them three or more times a week. For safety reasons and to get the most from your exercise, follow this routine: Warm up and stretch for the first 5 to 10 minutes. Exercise briskly for at least 20 minutes. Then, spend 5 minutes cooling down by exercising more slowly. Finish by stretching again, while your muscles are still warm.

Besides working out your heart and lungs, aerobic exercise burns sugars and fats. The

longer you exercise, the more you burn. But rest when you feel tired. If you're breathless, you are running out of oxygen and should stop to take in more.

When your body burns fuel, your temperature rises. Your body sweats to cool down. However, children don't sweat as much as adults. So if you run or bicycle for a while, break for a drink of water, or you may get overheated. Drinking water cools the body. It also replaces water that the body loses when it sweats.

Shape up and you'll be ready for anything— a sports game, a busy day, and a healthy life.

BODY BULLETIN

Breathing is an important part of exercising. Always exhale through your mouth during the most difficult part of the exercise. Then, inhale through your nose. For example, while doing pushups, breathe out when you push up, and breathe in when you lower your body.

BODYscience

Take a Body Break

Do you ever snack while you're watching TV? Some snacks give you fat and sugar, and sitting for a long time stiffens muscles. So, next time you watch TV, treat your body right. Take an exercise break.

1. While the opening credits roll, warm up your stiff muscles. Try jumping with an imaginary rope, circling your arms as you skip. When you're warmed up or start to sweat, stop and stretch.

2. To stretch many of your muscles, try a "shrink and grow" exercise. Stretch tall on tiptoe, reaching as high as you can. Then crouch down as low as possible, bending your knees and resting your weight on your heels. Stretch up and then down again.

3. To stretch your spine and leg muscles, sit on the floor with your legs straight out in front of you. Then, without leaning on your hands, "walk" your hands down your legs, from your thighs to your toes. (Keep your back straight.) When your hands are as far as they will go, hold that position for 15 seconds. Then walk them back up to your thighs. Do it again; try to go farther.

4. During commercials, strengthen your arms. First, lie facedown on the floor and place your palms shoulder-width apart. Then, slowly push up, supporting your body on your hands and knees. Next, slowly bend your arms to lower your body to the floor. Repeat as long as the commercials last. Remember: Keep your head and back in a straight line.

5. Strengthen your thighs while watching a show from a pretend chair against the wall. Put your back against the wall, walk your feet out a few inches, then stretch your arms in front of you. With your feet together and flat on the floor, slide down into a sitting position. Adjust your feet so that your knees are directly above your ankles, not in front of them or behind them. Sit in your pretend chair for 10 seconds. Rest, then try it again. After a few days of practice, try to sit for an entire commercial. The stronger your thigh muscles get, the longer you can hold this position.

Up with Soap

You have them on your fingers.
You have them in your hair.
Bacteria surround you.
You'll find them everywhere.

Your body is covered with bacteria. If some of them get inside you, they may make you sick. Then, when you sneeze or cough, germ-filled drops can enter the air and spread your sickness to other people.

Don't let bacteria get away with that. Fight back! After going to the bathroom, wash with soap and water to kill bacteria on your hands. Soap up again before meals to get rid of bacteria that might get on your food—and inside you.

Bacteria may even make you smell. They feed on the oil in your sweat. Then they multiply and die, causing an unpleasant odor. So every day, take a bath or shower or wash the places where you sweat the most, such as your feet and armpits.

BODY BULLETIN

Wearing natural fabrics–such as wool, cotton, and linen–helps stop body odor. Why? Because these fabrics absorb sweat from the skin, leaving bacteria without a food supply.

You must fight bacteria in the kitchen, too, because they spoil food. Spoiled food tastes and smells bad, and it may poison you if you eat it. Bits of spoiled food hide in such things as pans, can openers, and chopping boards. From there, bacteria can get into your food and into you. So wash, rinse, and dry kitchen tools after each use.

You can get rid of these bad types. Staying clean is half the battle. Just keep washing.

BODY LANGUAGE

Hygiene comes from the ancient Greeks' name for their goddess of health, Hygeia. Today we think of cleanliness when we hear the word *hygiene* because keeping clean discourages germs and disease.

Home Remedies

Doctors numbered few and far between in great-great-great-grandfather's time. He had to look after his family's health himself. Great Papa, which is what the family called him,

used the home remedies that had been handed down from his father. The recipes included herbs, roots, bark, and wild flowers, as well as some staples from the pantry shelf.

When Great Papa's wife, Abby, had an upset stomach, he steeped ginger in hot water. After a cup of ginger tea, Abby felt better. When his son, Isaac, had a stuffy nose, Great Papa made chicken soup with garlic for him. Isaac breathed more easily. When his daughter, Jane, couldn't sleep, Great Papa gave her warm milk. She fell asleep in minutes.

Scientists have since discovered why these home remedies work. Ginger appears to ease upset stomachs and motion sickness. Garlic in hot soup thins the mucus in your nose, helping clear a stuffy head. Warming up milk speeds its digestion, so its proteins quickly break down into smaller parts. One part called tryptophan (TRIHP tuh fan) helps your body produce chemicals that make you sleepy.

Here are some home remedies you can try:

🍃 Gargling with warm salt water soothes a sore throat.

🍃 Dab on a paste of baking soda and water to stop the itching from a mosquito bite.

🍃 Drinking a glass of tomato juice with seven drops of hot sauce helps you breathe easier when you have a cold.

🍃 Add a teaspoon of honey and a little lemon juice to a glass of warm water—drinking this soothes a sore throat. (Honey should not be given to babies less than a year old.)

🍃 After a meal, chew a bit of the herbs mint or parsley to sweeten your breath.

🍃 Spread a paste of warm oatmeal and water on your face (except around your eyes and mouth) to soothe hot, itchy skin.

Rest Your Head

WEE WILLIE WINKIE: Wee Willie Winkie here, the host of "Rest Your Head," the late-night show that talks you to sleep. Tonight we're on location in a ship in the sky. Let's meet our shipmates, the experts Wynken, Blynken, and Nod. Wynken, answer the question on all our minds: Why do we need sleep?

WYNKEN: Good question, Wee Willie. During sleep, your body's energy is restored, particularly in the brain and nervous system. You realize how much you need sleep when you go without it.

BLYNKEN: People who go without sleep for just one night have difficulty thinking and reasoning. They make more mistakes and react more slowly

than usual. They also tend to lose their temper more easily. After several nights without sleep, their behavior becomes even more unusual. They are also more likely to catch a cold or other illness because a tired body doesn't have energy to fight diseases.

WEE WILLIE WINKIE: How awful! Do they ever recover?

NOD: Yes, after one good night's sleep.

WEE WILLIE WINKIE: Nod, how do you suggest people get a good night's sleep?

NOD: Follow a routine. Go to bed at the same time each night and wake up at the same time each morning. Try not to sleep late on weekends. Oversleeping can keep you awake the next night.

201

BLYNKEN: Also, before bedtime, don't drink colas that have caffeine (KAF een). The caffeine makes your mind too alert to sleep.

WEE WILLIE WINKIE: Suppose you feel too tense to sleep. What can help you?

NOD: Exercise each day. Exercising helps relax your muscles. Don't exercise at bedtime, though. Right after a workout, the body usually wants to go, go, go, rather than sleep, sleep, sleep.

WYNKEN: Another way to relax is by laughing. Joke with a parent or read a funny book.

BLYNKEN: If you still can't sleep, think boring thoughts. Counting sheep really works. Try it.

WEE WILLIE WINKIE: One, two, three,

ZZZZZZZZZZZZZZZZ

Oops! What Do I Do Now?

Have you ever burned your hand or scraped your knee? Then you know that accidents happen. My name is Doctor Dana, and I have seen plenty of burns and scrapes. In fact, most of these types of accidents occur in the home, where people spend most of their time. That's why I'm visiting houses—to see which families are working to prevent accidents. These are the families that get the SAFETY OK.

First, be prepared—sometimes accidents happen no matter how careful you are. Check the family's first-aid kit with your mom or dad. Make certain the kit includes the following things: aspirin, eyebath (a sterile eye wash for washing chemicals out of the eye), cotton, adhesive tape, adhesive bandages, gauze bandages, an elastic bandage, a flashlight, latex gloves, a thermometer, a triangular bandage for slings, safety pins, scissors, tweezers, a cream for killing germs, a lotion for soothing itches, and a first-aid manual. It's also a good idea to keep towels and tissues nearby.

BODY BULLETIN

Check your garden for first-aid help? Sure! The thick leaves of certain aloe plants have a gel inside. Many people use the gel as a skin ointment, for example to soothe a sunburned nose.

Nobody can prevent all accidents, but there are many ways you and your family can work to have fewer of them. Take a safety walk around your house. What do you think could cause an accident?

Make sure family members take their time. Many accidents happen when people hurry and aren't careful about what they are doing.

Use a helmet and appropriate padding when biking or skating.

Keep harmful chemicals and poisons—such as bleach and weedkillers—where children can't get them and where they can't be confused with food. Store them in a high place or lock them up.

Check your yard for hidden holes or stakes that someone could trip in or over. Fill in the holes and remove the stakes.

Wear seat belts *every* time you're in a car.

To reach items on high shelves, always use a sturdy stepladder—never a chair.

A rubber mat in the tub and a rubber-backed rug on the floor will help keep you from slipping on a wet surface.

Shoes and toys should always be put away so that no one trips over them.

Pot handles should be over a counter or a cool burner—not in the walkway where they could be bumped, and not over a hot burner where they could get too hot to use.

Replace burned-out light bulbs right away. In dark places, people may trip.

Always practice the "walk with the points down" rule. Whenever you carry something that has a point—such as scissors or a sharpened pencil—walk with the point down so it won't hurt you or somebody else.

Some accidents require a doctor's help, but others can be handled by you and a grown-up. The following chart gives you tips on how to handle certain emergencies with the help of a grown-up. Copy the chart and keep the copy with your first-aid kit.

Emergency	What to Do	Get help...
Tooth knocked out	Try to place the tooth back in your mouth. If this isn't possible, quickly place the tooth in a glass of milk. The milk keeps the many tiny ligaments around the root of the tooth moist and may help keep the tooth alive.	to go to the dentist or to the hospital. The dentist may be able to put the tooth back in if you get there quickly.
Object in your ear	Do not stick anything in your ear. Tilt your head to the side to make the object fall out.	to go to the emergency room if the object does not fall out, if it was pointed, or if your ear is bleeding.
Poison ivy	Wash thoroughly with soap and water right away. Wash clothes and anything else that touched the plant—or anything you rubbed against after touching the plant—so as not to spread the oils further.	to cover the rash with lotion that will stop the itching.
Scrape	Wash your hands. Then clean the scrape with soap and water. Rinse well.	to bandage the scrape if it is bleeding.
Small bleeding cut	If the cut bleeds a little, wash your hands and then wash the cut. Then press a clean cloth against the cut to stop the bleeding. If the cut bleeds a lot, press against it to stop the bleeding before you wash it.	from a grown-up to apply an adhesive bandage. If the bleeding continues, see a doctor.
Bruise	Apply a cold, wet cloth to the bruise to ease the pain and swelling.	to apply a bandage if your clothes are rubbing against the bruise.

Emergency	What to Do	Get help...
Mosquito, gnat, or fly bite	Do not scratch the bite. Wash it with soap and water. Cover any swelling with a cold, wet cloth.	to soothe the itch with a lotion.
Foot, calf, or hand cramp	Straighten your leg and gently pull your toes toward you to get rid of a cramp in your foot or calf. Gently bend your fingers backward to relieve a cramp in your hand.	from a grown-up if the cramp continues.
Small burn	If there is no mark, or just a red spot no bigger than the palm of your hand, run cold tap water over it for about 10 minutes to ease the pain. (If the water feels too cold, take it out briefly.) Then, gently blot the area dry.	from a grown-up to bandage the burn to keep out dirt.
Bumped head	Sit for a minute to get your bearings because your body is probably stunned from the jolt.	to cover the bump with a towel soaked in cold water if there is swelling. An adult can also check to be sure that you are speaking and seeing clearly.

Remember, when you get hurt, always tell an adult right away, no matter how small you think the accident might be. Swift action in an emergency is important.

BO**D**Y**science**

All Body Systems Go!

THINGS YOU NEED:

- several sheets
  of paper
- scissors
- 1 pencil or pen
  for each player
- a small bowl

1. Cut a sheet of paper
into 15 slips. On each
slip, write a number
from 1 to 15. Put the
slips in the bowl.

2. Draw a slip of paper. Match its
number with the corresponding
question on page 210 or 211.
On your answer sheet, write the
number of the question and your
answer. Put the slip aside.

3. If you play with friends, take turns
drawing. If you play alone,
continue pulling slips.

4. After all the slips are drawn,
compare your answers with the
ones on page 209. (Refer to the
appropriate section of the book
for more details.) Count the points
you earn for each correct answer.
The player with the most points
wins. If you play alone, play again
and try to beat your score.

Variations: After drawing a slip, have each person try to write
8 facts about the topic listed in the corresponding space on page
210 or 211. Or, make up questions for your friend, and have your
friend make up some for you. Have the questions correspond to
the topics listed in the numbered spaces on pages 210 and 211.

1. Answer: false
   You use muscles even when standing still. If they weren't working, you would collapse in a heap!
   2 points
2. Answer: They can make you tired and overweight. Fats also can give you bad cholesterol.
   3 points
3. Answer: no part
   The bronchi and bronchioles in your lungs have some muscles, but they don't push the air out. The muscles in your chest wall and the diaphragm below the lungs do the work.
   2 points
4. Answer: lack of oxygen
   As a red blood cell gives its oxygen to other body cells, it turns dull or bluish. It picks up more oxygen in the lungs.
   1 point
5. Answer: The cytoplasm is the jellylike fluid inside the cell. The nucleus is the control center. The selectively permeable membrane is the cell's thin covering.
   2 points
6. Answer: an allergy
   Some people are unusually sensitive, or allergic, to certain substances. For example, some people break out in hives when they eat foods such as shrimp or strawberries.
   2 points
7. Answer: about 50 gallons (189.3 liters)
   The kidneys monitor salt and water levels and send wastes to the bladder.
   3 points
8. Answer: false
   Muscles do the pushing. That's why you can swallow while you are upside down.
   1 point
9. Answer: freckles
   Sunlight causes the skin in those spots to produce more of the dark pigment called melanin.
   2 points
10. Answer: cones
    Cones are receptor cells in the lining of each eye that help you see colors in bright light. Rods help you see black, white, and gray, and they help you see in dim light.
    3 points
11. Answer: the bottom of your brain stem, your medulla oblongata
    The brain stem also controls your digestive and circulatory systems.
    2 points
12. Answer: the pituitary gland
    This endocrine gland controls many other glands in your body and the release of hormones.
    2 points
13. Answer: to help digestion
    Bile is sent to the small intestine to help break down and absorb fat.
    2 points
14. Answer: the stirrup bone inside the ear
    This bone measures about 1/10 inch (.25 centimeter) long.
    3 points
15. Answer: aspirin, eyebath, cotton, adhesive tape, adhesive bandages, gauze bandages, an elastic bandage, a flashlight, latex gloves, a thermometer, a triangular bandage for slings, safety pins, scissors, tweezers, a cream for killing germs, a lotion for soothing itches, a first-aid manual
    1 point for each item named

**DON'T PEEK!
READ PAGES 208,
210, AND 211 FIRST.**

Muscles
1. True or False: Your muscles don't do any work when you're standing still.

Skin
9. What do you call clumps of melanin in the skin?

Digestive System
13. Why does your liver make bile?

Nervous System
11. Which part of your brain controls breathing?

Urinary System
7. On the average, how many gallons of blood do kidneys filter each day?

Senses
10. Which cells in your eyes help you see colors?

Immune System
6. What do you have when your antibodies attack a substance that is harmless to many other people?

Breathing
3. Which part of the lungs pushes air out?

Glands
12. Which body part is known as the "top gland"?

Skeleton
14. What is the smallest bone in your body?

Health
2. How are too much sugar and fat bad for you?

Digestive System
8. True or False: Gravity pushes food down into your stomach.

Safety
15. How many items can you name that belong in a first-aid kit?

Cells
5. Name and describe two parts of a cell.

Circulatory System
4. What makes red blood cells dull or bluish?

A Ten-Step Body Plan

What are you doing to make a stronger, healthier, happier you? Try out this super-duper plan. Add at least one new step to your routine each week.

1 Learn to play an instrument or to sing. Practicing any new skill develops a new area of the brain and increases your brainpower.

2 Stand and sit up straight. Good posture makes body parts work better and makes you feel better.

3 Give yourself a manicure for healthy hands. Ask a grown-up to show you how to clean and file nails, and how to push back your cuticles.

4 Eat different kinds of raw vegetables with low-fat dip. Your digestive system will like the fiber.

Finish

10 Give and get hugs. Studies show that babies who are cuddled and talked to are happier and healthier. It's good for you, too.

8 Treat your nose. Tour a spice cabinet, or help a grown-up bake a loaf of bread. Then breathe deeply and smell the aroma.

9 Walk in a forest preserve or tree-lined park. Trees give off clean oxygen, so you can truly take a breath of fresh air.

7 Get good at one aerobic activity to strengthen your heart and lungs. For example, perfect a jump-rope routine, increase your walking speed, become an expert hiker in your neighborhood, or join a martial arts or dance class.

5 Drink plenty of water. Water helps flush wastes from your body.

6 Stay away from smoking, of course, but also avoid second-hand smoke as much as possible.

Books to Read

Check your school or public library for more books about your amazing body. Here are some titles you're sure to enjoy:

Ages 5-8

A Book About Your Skeleton
by Ruth Belov Gross (Scholastic, 1994)
◆ Bright, splashy pictures and easy-to-read words introduce the youngest readers to what their skeleton does for them.

The Brain: What It Is, What It Does
by Ruth Dowling Bruun and Bertel Bruun (Greenwillow, 1989)
◆ Learn more about "brain central" with this brainy book.

First Questions and Answers About the Human Body: What Is a Bellybutton?
(Time-Life Books, 1993)
◆ This question-and-answer book treats fascinating details about the human body with easy-to-understand writing and fine illustrations.

How I Breathe
by Mandy Suhr (Carolrhoda, 1992)
◆ Find out about that most basic function of all—breathing—told through a child's voice and simply illustrated. Similar books by the author include *I Am Growing*, *When I Eat*, and *I Can Move*.

How You Were Born
by Joanna Cole (Morrow, 1993)
◆ Follow the story of a baby's journey into the world when you read this beautifully written and illustrated book.

Keeping Clean
by Vicki Cobb (Lippincott, 1989)
◆ What would happen if you didn't keep yourself clean? This fun book tells you. It includes cartoon drawings and a look at how people have tried to stay clean in the past.

Look at Your Eyes
by Paul Showers (HarperCollins, 1992)
◆ Look at your eyes and see how you see. That's what the boy in this story does. Other good books by this author include *What Happens to a Hamburger?* and *A Drop of Blood*.

The Magic School Bus Inside the Human Body
by Joanna Cole (Scholastic, 1989)
◆ How can Ms. Frizzle's second-graders actually take a school bus ride inside a human body? Read and find out!

Outside and Inside You
by Sandra Markle (Bradbury, 1991)
◆ Take a peek inside yourself through the pictures and explanations about the human body in this book.

The Senses: A Lift-the-Flap Body Book
by Angela Royston (Barron's, 1993)
◆ Lift the flaps and try some simple experiments to learn more about your senses.

Ages 8-12

The Body Atlas
by Steve Parker (Dorling Kindersley, 1993)
◆ Take a head-to-toe look at the human body with this amazing "atlas" containing marvelous illustrations.

Cell Wars
by Fran Balkwill (Carolrhoda, 1993)
◆ Find out how hard cells work for you in fighting disease. *Cells Are Us*, another book by this author, is a fine introduction to cells and has excellent pictures.

Down the Hatch: Find Out About Your Food
by Mike Lambourne (Millbrook, 1992)
◆ Facts, pictures, and cartoons about digestion are presented in this fun book about the body.

Eat the Right Stuff: Food Facts
by Catherine Reef (Twenty-First Century, 1993)
◆ Get the facts about what to eat and why with this helpful guide. Also by this author is *Stay Fit: Build a Strong Body*.

How Do We Dream? And Other Questions About Your Body
by Jack Myers (Boyds Mills, 1992)
◆ Dreaming is only one of many wonders discussed in this question-and-answer book. Find out about laughing, salty tears, snoring, and lots of other amazing body facts.

How the Body Works
by Steve Parker (Reader's Digest, 1994)
◆ See if your parent or teacher can help you try some of the experiments in this beautifully illustrated book.

The Mystery of Sleep
by Alvin and Virginia Silverstein (Little, Brown, 1987)
◆ Your brain's still at work while you're sleeping. Find out how, and learn about sleep problems, too.

The Pulse of Life: The Circulatory System
by Jenny Bryan (Dillon, 1993)
◆ Different heart and blood topics, beautifully pictured, make up this book. Also by the author is *Breathing: The Respiratory System*.

The Visual Dictionary of the Human Body
(Dorling Kindersley, 1991)
◆ Don't miss *The Visual Dictionary*! Its outstanding illustrations will capture your attention right away, and the labels and text will clearly explain the body.

What Makes You What You Are: A First Look at Genetics
by Sandy Bornstein (Messner, 1989)
◆ Find out about your genes at work. Activities are included as well.

New Words

Here are some words you have read in this book. Some may be new to you. You can see how to say them in the parentheses after the word, for example: **antibody** (AN tee BAHD ee). Say the parts in small letters in your normal voice, those in small capital letters a little louder, and those in large capital letters loudest. Following the pronunciation are one or two sentences that tell the word's meaning as it is used in this book.

noo wurdz

antibody (AN tee BAHD ee) A kind of protein that helps destroy harmful substances in your body. Antibodies are produced by white blood cells.

aorta (ay AWR tuh) The largest artery in your body. It carries blood from the left side of your heart.

bile (byl) A digestive juice that helps your body break down and absorb fats. Bile is produced in your liver and stored in your gallbladder.

carbohydrate (KAHR boh HY drayt) A nutrient that supplies your body with fuel. Simple sugars, starches, and fibers are types of carbohydrates.

cardiac (KAHR dee ak) Describing the muscle of the heart; or having to do with the heart.

cartilage (KAHR tuh lihj) Tough, flexible tissue. Cartilage makes up parts of your nose, ears, and ribcage.

cell (sehl) A tiny living unit of your body. Cells are the building blocks of all living things.

cerebellum (SEHR uh BEHL uhm) The part of your brain that controls muscle coordination. It lies below the back part of your cerebrum.

cerebrum (SEHR uh bruhm) The largest part of your brain. It is divided into two hemispheres.

chromosome (KROH muh sohm) A structure in a cell's nucleus that is made largely of DNA and proteins.

cilia (SIHL ee uh) Tiny hairlike structures in your nose, trachea, and bronchi. Cilia help sweep out harmful substances.

contract (kuhn TRAKT) To get smaller or shorter and thicker. Muscles contract to move body parts.

cortex (KOHR tehks) In the brain, the outer part, or gray matter,

of the cerebrum is called the cortex. In hair, the layer between the medulla and the cuticle is also called the cortex.

dermis (DUHR mihs) The middle layer of your skin. The dermis contains blood vessels, nerve endings, sweat glands, oil glands, and hair follicles.

diaphragm (DY uh fram) The large muscle that lies below your lungs on the bottom of your chest cavity.

dilate (DY layt) To expand, or become larger.

DNA (DEE EHN AY) A substance within chromosomes that contains genes, instructions for your body's cells. DNA stands for *d*eoxyribo*n*ucleic *a*cid.

esophagus (ee SAHF uh guhs) The long tube that connects your mouth and stomach.

gene (jeen) A section of DNA. It carries instructions for a particular characteristic, such as eye color or height.

heredity (huh REH duh tee) The passing of traits from parents to offspring.

hormone (HOHR mohn) Usually produced by an endocrine gland, a hormone travels through the blood to regulate functions elsewhere in the body.

hypothalamus (HY puh THAL uh muhs) The part of the brain that controls the pituitary gland.

larynx (LAIR ihngks) The box-shaped structure at the top of the trachea. It helps you speak and is sometimes called the voice box.

lymphocyte (LIHM fuh syt) A type of white blood cell that is largely made in the lymph nodes and that produces antibodies.

marrow (MAIR oh) The soft, jellylike substance inside your bones. Yellow marrow is mainly fat. Red marrow produces blood cells.

mucus (MYOO kuhs) A sticky, slimy fluid found in many parts of your body. In your nose, it helps trap harmful substances. In your lungs, it helps keep alveoli moist.

neuron (NOOR ahn) A nerve cell.

neutrophil (NOO truh fihl) A type of white blood cell. It attacks harmful organisms by engulfing them and eating them.

nucleus (NOO klee uhs) The control center of a cell.

opposable thumb (uh POHZ uh buhl thuhm) A thumb that can be placed opposite the other fingers of the hand. The joints of the thumb bend toward the other fingers to grasp things and to make delicate motions.

organ (OHR guhn) Any part of the body that is made up of two or more kinds of tissue and performs a specific job. The heart is an organ.

pancreas (PAN kree uhs) An organ that helps you digest food. It produces chemicals that break down proteins, change starches to sugars, and break apart fats.

peristalsis (PEHR uh STAL sihs) Wavelike contractions of the esophagus, stomach, or other organ through which substances are moved.

pituitary gland (pih TOO uh TEHR ee gland) A small endocrine gland—known as "Top Gland"—in your brain. It produces hormones and controls many other endocrine glands.

plasma (PLAZ muh) The yellowish clear liquid that makes up more than half of your blood. Plasma is mostly water.

platelet (PLAYT liht) A small blood cell that helps heal cuts by aiding blood clotting.

protein (PROH teen) A nutrient your body needs. It is one of the main building blocks of cells.

receptor (rih SEHP tuhr) A nerve ending that receives a certain kind of sensory message, such as light rays, heat, or touch.

selectively permeable (sih LEHK tihv lee PUHR mee uh buhl) Allowing some things to pass through, but not others. A cell membrane is selectively permeable.

specialize (SPEHSH uh lyz) To become different from one another; to become able to do specific tasks.

striation (stry AY shuhn) A light or dark band on a muscle fiber. Voluntary skeletal muscles have striations. Involuntary smooth muscles do not.

synapse (sih NAPS) A tiny space between nerve cells. Messages are sent across synapses from one nerve cell to another.

tendon (TEHN duhn) A strong cord that attaches a muscle to a bone.

tissue (TIHSH yoo) A group of similar cells working together, such as muscle cells in muscle tissue.

trachea (TRAY kee uh) The tube through which air travels from your nose and mouth to your lungs. It is also called the windpipe.

vocal cords (VOH kuhl kohrdz) Folds of elastic tissue in your larynx. When air passes through the larynx, they vibrate and contract to help you speak.

Illustration Acknowledgments

The publishers of *Childcraft* gratefully acknowledge the courtesy of the following illustrators, photographers, agencies, and organizations for illustrations in this volume. When all the illustrations for a sequence of pages are from a single source, the inclusive page numbers are given. Credits should be read from left to right, top to bottom, on their respective pages. All illustrations are the exclusive property of the publishers of *Childcraft* unless names are marked with an asterisk (*).

Index

This index is an alphabetical list of important topics covered in this book. It will help you find information given in both words and pictures. To help you understand what an entry means, there is sometimes a helping word in parentheses, for example, **anatomy** (science). If there is information in both words and pictures, you will see the words *with pictures* in parentheses after the page number. If there is only a picture, you will see the word *picture* in parentheses after the page number.

World Book Encyclopedia, Inc. provides high quality educational and reference products for the family and school, including a FIVE-VOLUME CHILDCRAFT FAVORITES SET, colorful books on favorite topics, such as DOGS and PREHISTORIC ANIMALS; and THE WORLD BOOK/RUSH-PRESBYTERIAN-ST. LUKE'S MEDICAL CENTER MEDICAL ENCYCLOPEDIA, a 1,072-page, fully illustrated family health reference. For further information, write WORLD BOOK ENCYCLOPEDIA, INC., P.O. Box 3073, Evanston, IL 60204-3073.